CATASTROPHE
IN THE MAKING

Catastrophe

in the

Making

—◆—

*The Engineering of Katrina
and the Disasters of Tomorrow*

—◆—

William R. Freudenburg
Robert Gramling
Shirley Laska
Kai T. Erikson

● **ISLAND**PRESS / Shearwater Books
Washington | Covelo | London

A Shearwater Book
Published by Island Press

Copyright © 2009 Willliam R. Freudenburg, Robert B. Gramling,
Shirley B. Laska, and Kai T. Erikson

SHEARWATER BOOKS is a trademark of The Center for Resource Economics.

Library of Congress Cataloging-in-Publication Data
Freudenburg, William R.
Catastrophe in the making : the engineering of Katrina and the disasters of
tomorrow / William R. Freudenburg, Robert B. Gramling, Shirley B. Laska.
p. cm.
Includes bibliographical references and index.
ISBN-13: 978-1-59726-682-6 (cloth : alk. paper)
ISBN-10: 1-59726-682-5 (cloth : alk. paper)
1. Hurricane Katrina, 2005. 2. Hurricane protection—Louisiana—
Evaluation. 3. Flood control—Louisiana—New Orleans—Evaluation.
4. Levees—Louisiana—New Orleans—History. 5. Levees—Mississippi
River. 6. Emergency management—Louisiana—New Orleans. 7. Economic
development—Environmental aspects—Louisiana—New Orleans.
I. Gramling, Robert B. II. Laska, Shirley Bradway, 1944- III. Title.
HV636 2005 .N4 F74 2009   363.34'9220976090511—dc22
2009021516

British Cataloging-in-Publication data available.
Printed on recycled, acid-free paper ✪

Design by David Bullen

Manufactured in the United States of America

10   9   8   7   6   5   4   3   2   1

Keywords: Army Corps of Engineers, Federal Emergency Management Agency (FEMA),
Mississippi River Gulf Outlet (MRGO), natural hazards, environmental justice,
city planning, wetlands, floodwall, storm surge

To all who have suffered
needlessly from "natural" disasters,
and to future citizens
who may not need to suffer if we begin to act now.

Contents

Prologue   The First Days of Katrina   *3*

Chapter 1   A Mighty Storm Hits the Shore   *15*

Chapter 2   The Setting   *31*

Chapter 3   Slicing Through the Swamps   *45*

Chapter 4   The Growth Machine Comes to New Orleans   *55*

Chapter 5   A "Helpful Explosion"   *67*

Chapter 6   The Collapse of Engineered Systems   *91*

Chapter 7   The Loss of Natural Defenses   *111*

Chapter 8   Critical for Economic Survival?   *135*

Chapter 9   The Axe in the Attic   *147*

Chapter 10   The End of an Error?   *163*

              Endnotes   *171*

              References   *183*

              Acknowledgments   *197*

              Index   *201*

Catastrophe
in the
Making

Prologue

The First Days of Katrina

*T*HE STAGGERING DISASTER we have come to call "Katrina"
was named for a hurricane that formed out in the vastness of
the Atlantic Ocean in the waning days of August 2005.

It began as a barely noticeable wisp of wind. The waters were
unusually warm even for that time of year, and as moist air was drawn
up into the shifting winds above, a number of modest thunderstorms
began to form and then, gradually, to merge into a larger and more
continuous weather system. All this happens many times in the
course of a single season.

As this particular weather system grew in size, it began to rotate
slowly, and in doing so, it soon began to suck up more and more moisture from the surface of the ocean below. That moisture, once aloft,
was quickly converted into rain, and as textbooks explain, this con-
densation added further warmth to the process. In a way, the weather
system was beginning to look and behave like a living creature—it
was developing its own life force. It had become a self-reinforcing
spiral that generated its own momentum and its own energy.

The system was designated "tropical depression twelve" of the 2005
season as it gathered force in waters to the south and east of the
Bahamas. It was upgraded to tropical storm status and given its code
name by the morning of August 24, making that the one and only
day of Tropical Storm Katrina. The mass was now worth watching,

but still, such storms can occur more than a dozen times in the course of a season.

By the next day, the storm had become a hurricane, making that day, August 25, the first day of Hurricane Katrina. Technically, "hurricanes" are tropical cyclones in the North Atlantic with wind speeds in excess of 74 miles per hour. They draw their energy from the warmth of the waters below, and as a consequence of the earth's own rotation as it moves through space, they take on a strange and often terrifying spin, which in the Northern Hemisphere churns counterclockwise. Hurricanes, of course, are serious things. Over the past century, we have rarely seen more than half a dozen of them in a single year.

Hurricanes bring with them fierce winds, lashing rains, and, most lethally, punishing storm surges. Unlike a tsunami, which is a wave that suddenly shoots across an otherwise calm sea, a storm surge is more like an abnormally high tide, an enormous rise in the height of the ocean itself, on the top of which the winds build waves, which worsen the destruction as they crash into the shore. In sum, the storm surge consists of battering waves riding atop a concentrated, terrible mass of water.

The surges that usually do the greatest harm are those caused by the "right hook" of the swirling storm, where the winds, racing around their own core, are at the same time propelled forward by the trajectory of the storm itself. As the winds spiral in a counterclockwise direction past what would be six on the face of a clock, and then circle full bore toward three, the clock face itself is moving forward—in effect further increasing the speed of the winds, and worse, driving them across open water and directly toward the land.

Up until that point, when people on shore had just begun to worry about the storm and charting its path, Katrina was little more than a minor footnote in meteorological history. It had entered the record only the day before, when it was given its code name. Just two hours after it officially became a hurricane, though, Katrina made its first real appearance in human history when it swept across the southern tip of Florida, causing several deaths and doing a billion dollars' worth of property damage.

While Katrina dealt a serious blow to Florida—only about two dozen hurricanes have ever wreaked that much damage to the United

States—the initial salvo would be dwarfed by Katrina's later destruction. By itself, however, the destructive path across Florida would not have left anything like Katrina's lasting mark, and in some ways, it could have been good news for the rest of the Gulf. Hurricanes lose intensity when their momentum carries them across land, in part because the irregular surface of the land acts as a kind of brake, and in part because the winds themselves tend to lose some of their ferocity when they are cut off from the warm, storm-invigorating waters of the sea.[1]

That is what happened to Katrina, too, as it blew across Florida, but it remained an official if weaker hurricane, and its force was renewed as it reentered the warm waters of the Gulf of Mexico, an hour before sunrise on August 26—the second day of Hurricane Katrina. Those storm-intensifying waters were the warmest ever registered in a hundred years of record keeping, and as Katrina churned relentlessly across the Gulf during its third day, it grew ominously in size and intensity. On the fourth day, as Katrina coiled for its assault on the coastline of Louisiana, it had become a massive Category 5 hurricane on the Saffir-Simpson scale, filling nearly the entire Gulf. It was, at that time, the strongest hurricane ever recorded in the Gulf of Mexico.[2]

Katrina weakened somewhat on its fifth day as a hurricane, dropping to a Category 3 storm just before making landfall, but it was still sustaining winds of 125 miles per hour and driving a monstrous storm surge. By 6:00 in the morning of August 29, the storm was battering the Mississippi River Delta community of Buras, Louisiana, virtually sweeping it away. Soon afterward, Katrina crossed Breton Sound, to the east of New Orleans, making landfall once again with winds of 120 miles an hour. Within the next few hours, it would become the costliest disaster in American history, and one of the deadliest.

A Hurricane Ends, a Disaster Begins

This was also a critical period in the brief career of the hurricane named Katrina, for it was here that the storm began the extraordinary path of devastation that would carry it across the delta, into New Orleans, and beyond. Further, it was during those early morning hours of August 29 that Katrina crossed the line that separated empty sea from settled land and entered human history with a vengeance. In a sense, the hurricane arrived on the scene and began to dissipate just as the true history of "Katrina" was about to begin. The storm was but a preliminary to the main event, even though it provided the name by which the main event will probably always be known. Hurricane Katrina was, indeed, a prologue.

The transition from sea to land, we may presume, did not matter to Katrina. The hurricane was as oblivious to what it was doing to the ground below as to what it had done to the surface waters of the Gulf. But as we try to come to terms with what followed, it is important to understand that what we so casually describe as a "natural" disaster is really a collision between some cataclysmic force of nature—a wind, a tide, a quake, a conflagration—and a human habitat located in harm's way. It is the character of the habitat being struck rather than the character of the force doing the striking that we study to get the true measure of the disaster. In the case of Katrina, the storm sliced into a complex human landscape, and the calamity that followed will be remembered not for the velocity of its winds or the size of its storm surges, but for the amount of damage it did to the landscape and to the humans who inhabited it.

We are not speaking of "natural" happenings here in any of the familiar meanings of the term. We are speaking of human beings— their strengths and fragilities, their resources and limitations, their resiliencies and rigidities—and human constructs. If Katrina had made landfall on an unoccupied shore somewhere else in the world— if it had uprooted trees, gouged up the land itself, redrawn the contours of the coastline, and otherwise rearranged the landscape—few if any reporters of the news would have considered it a "disaster." Few would even have considered it "news." The real wreckage of Katrina was not in damage done to the countryside, but in ruined lives, collapsed social orders, and crushed dreams.

We open the book in this manner to make a critical point. Everything that came before the storm hit land, as we have been at pains to suggest, was prologue, which is why we entitled these introductory remarks as we did. To understand a disaster like Katrina, though, one must look at three quite separate stories.

In human terms, this prologue—the storm itself—is merely the precipitating event, the first but by far the least important of the three stories. The intensity of a storm that churns across open water may generate a certain interest among meteorologists, but for our purposes, that first story can now be left behind.

The second story began the moment when the hurricane came ashore. As we have suggested, this second story is about what happened when the storm entered human history; it involves the environmental, social, and human effects of the precipitating event on the landscape it visited. This second story is about human actions and consequences, not about natural forces. It is the story of the harm that a natural cataclysm can inflict on human lives, human structures, and human ways of thinking and doing. That devastation is what most of us picture in our minds when we remember Katrina, and it is what most of the books and articles with "Katrina" in their titles have been about. They deal with things that happened during and after the winds calmed and the floodwaters slipped back into the sea. They deal with effects, consequences, aftermaths.

It is the third story, however, that we regard as most critical in understanding the nature of human disasters, and it is mainly this third story that this book is really about. This missing third story is actually the earliest, taking us back in time—before the years of suffering and uncertainty and sorrow that followed the storm, before landfall, and before the storm system began to form.

So long as we analyze Katrina simply in terms of the other two stories, we will continue to think of it the way most have been tempted to think of it to date—a case of nature striking humans. If we are truly to understand what happened to the New Orleans region, however, it is important to understand those other two stories in the context of the third. It is from the perspective of the third story that we can begin to learn that Katrina was actually a case of humans having first struck nature—doing so with consequences that would come back to haunt us all.

What happened to New Orleans is not a story about the way natural forces sometimes hammer us. Rather, it is a story about the way humans can rearrange the contours of the land they settle on, doing so in ways that make it, and hence themselves, more vulnerable and exposed—inadvertent authors of their own distress.

It only takes a slight shift in thinking, a minor readjustment in focus, to see disasters in that light. If we are to understand the San Francisco earthquake and fire of 1906, for example, we would be well advised to concentrate not on the force of the tremors as measured on the Richter scale, or the heat of the flames as measured in degrees, but on how the city itself had been constructed and managed, how the life there was patterned before disaster struck. Similarly, if we are to understand the tsunami that devastated the coasts of South Asia in 2004, we would be well advised to focus not on the height of the tidal wave as it came ashore or the volume of water it brought with it, but on the prior removal of the mangrove trees that had long shielded the coast, and on the ways in which people and homes and roadways and essential institutions had been arrayed in the path of the wave. The same is true for Katrina.

This third story of Katrina, however, has connections not just to other disasters but also to the times and tempos we see as ordinary. Almost by definition, to refer to "disasters" is to refer to some of the rarest events of human history, and we reinforce that convention here by recalling other famous events—earthquakes, tsunamis—that are commonly seen as "disastrous." Still, Katrina may have just as many connections to what we call "normal."

As noted long ago by Kenneth Hewitt, a thoughtful student of disasters, the convention in our language is to describe disasters as being so far removed from the patterns of everyday life that they are "un" events—not just unfortunate, but uncommon, unexpected, unplanned, uncontrollable. We think of them as sudden shocks, noteworthy in part because they are so far removed from everything we think of as common, expected, and planned. Disasters are thus a kind of parenthetical insertion, located within the ordinary sweep of events but kept conceptually separate nevertheless. As conventionally understood, a "disaster" begins with a sudden spurt of misbehavior from natural systems that are otherwise far more orderly—the shaking of formerly solid earth, the arrival of a fast-moving tsunami, the moment when a hurricane slams into land. They end with the arrival of the people we call "the authorities," who announce that the natural misbehaviors have ended and that humans are once again in charge—starting the process of bringing back the patterns that we think of as being normal or ordinary and hence reassuring.[3]

What many have seen as remarkable about Katrina is the problematic nature of the closing parenthesis—the fact that the authorities took so long to arrive, and that they showed such stunning levels of incompetence once they got there. Fair enough; we will spend much less time on those topics than most "Katrina books," and in any case we will have little to say that would contradict those earlier observations. Where we differ is in thinking about the opening parenthesis, which in our way of thinking belongs much earlier. In what has become the traditional telling of the Katrina saga, the central conclusions have to do with uniqueness—the unusual power of the storm, meteorologically speaking, or the extraordinary ineffectiveness of the authorities' responses. By contrast, when seen from the perspective of the third story of Katrina, which goes furthest back in time, the experiences of New Orleans are better seen as shared, rather than unique, and as having a lot to teach the rest of us about what we have come to see as "normal."

That relevance is particularly important in a time of growing human influence over patterns we once called "natural." If the standard story of a disaster begins suddenly, when nature delivers a sharp and unexpected body blow to humans, this larger third story of Katrina stretches across a period of decades or even centuries, during which we humans have been delivering our own blows to nature. For the most part, those blows have been delivered in a way that is far more gradual than the striking of a storm, and far from having been distinct from the ordinary flow of human events, the key human actions that helped to create the Katrina disaster have long been regarded as ordinary. In the end, though, the consequences of the human blows to nature were what proved to be the most disastrous.

As we will spell out in the pages that follow, the most important of those human actions, in terms of their potential for disaster, were those that were carried out in the name of economic growth, albeit seldom with that actual outcome. A hurricane did indeed bring lashing winds and raging waters to New Orleans, but in the end it was the human landscape, made vulnerable by the acts of humans—especially a small number of business-oriented humans—that turned out to be the central character in this third story of Katrina.

In discussing this point, we will refer to what social scientists call "The Growth Machine"—a set of dynamics that tends to shape the daily economic life of most American communities. As generally understood, the term refers to a process that is built and set in motion by persons who focus on profit and "progress," but one that has no internal brakes and no sensors to take note of the damage it is doing as it churns along. Significantly, the people who work hardest to energize the Growth Machine are usually seen not as villains, but as community leaders.

There are good reasons why they enjoy such a reputation, and their efforts to promote "economic growth" will generally enjoy reasonably widespread support from other citizens in their communities. The danger lies not so much in their overall goals as in the specific ways in which those goals are pursued—and in the longer-term consequences of their efforts. The problem is that, like some twisted variation on the Peter Principle, the Growth Machine can move relentlessly ahead until it reaches its own level of incompetence. Key agents of the Growth Machine—engineers and developers and speculators—rarely ask what their limitations are. They assume that they can reshape the natural world in any manner that profits them; often, they continue to think so until the momentum of some venture carries them across that outer line and they come face to face with disaster on the other side.[4]

In emphasizing the ways in which New Orleans resembles the rest of the nation, rather than how it differs, we will be departing from the examples established by many of the city's best-known analysts. In particular, some highly respected American geographers and historians—Peirce Lewis and Ari Kelman offering distinguished examples—have emphasized the paradoxes of New Orleans' physical location. On the one hand, if one takes into account the way the Mississippi River has carved its path to the sea, and the ways in which the rest of the terrain in that part of the world has been shaped by nature, then New Orleans has always been located in one of the most compelling locations to be found on the map. In the technical talk of geographers, this aspect of city location was long ago named "situation"—and in Kelman's telling, New Orleans has a "near-perfect situation." At the same time, they argue, the location of New Orleans is one of the worst "sites" to be found anywhere—by which they mean that the ground underfoot is a bit less solid than in most places, as well as being more vulnerable to the kind of damage delivered by Hurricane Katrina. Lewis refers to the site on which New Orleans lies as "impossible" and "wretched," while Kelman describes New Orleans as "the nation's most improbable metropolis," located on "an almost unimaginably bad site."[5]

The point both of them are making is that a great contrast exists between the "near-perfect" location of New Orleans—particularly its relationship, for purposes of commerce and trade, to other places on the map—and the wretchedness of the site itself. This contrast has led to an energetic and ingenious brand of landscape engineering, intended to "overcome the hazards" of the site and, in effect, to improve upon the flaws imposed by nature. All of this is quite consistent with the argument you will read in the following chapters, and indeed we learned a good deal from those distinguished observers. The question we want to raise, however, goes a step further, asking why so many of the energetic and ingenious applications of engineering in this region have had the long-term effect of rendering that "wretched" site so much more fragile than it had been before.

There are two profoundly important reasons for understanding New Orleans in this way. The first and most obvious is that any recovery plan for the city that does not take that history into account is almost sure to fail. The second is that, for all its uniqueness from a cultural and social standpoint, New Orleans is by no means unique in the ways in which local leaders have increased their communities' vulnerability to "natural" disasters. For that reason, it can serve the rest of the country as a very important object lesson, almost a kind of parable. Millions of us live in places that share vulnerabilities with New Orleans, even if they do not share its music and cuisine and other cultural graces. In that sense, we are all from New Orleans, and the Katrinas that lurk on the other side of the horizon threaten us all.

What Is to Follow

In Chapter 1, we briefly recount what Hurricane Katrina did to both town and countryside after it moved across the coastline and into human history. This is the usual terrain of the second story of Katrina, and as just noted, it has received enough attention from others that we will visit it only briefly. In so doing, we will take note of how the story was initially reported in the news and how it has since been dealt with by sociologists, geographers, and historians, although we will also bring in some aspects and images of the story that are less well known, involving the ways in which the disaster was experienced by the authors of this book and by some of our friends and colleagues.

Chapter 2 takes us back to beginnings: the ways in which natural forces shaped the Mississippi Delta in geological time and in which native peoples and later visitors settled it in historical time.

Chapter 3 begins to tell what we are calling "the third story" of Katrina—the one that has received the least attention so far. This chapter describes the early (and sometimes awkward) efforts of the original settlers of New Orleans to "improve" upon the landscape left to them by the forces of nature—often by cutting canals across the surfaces of the land in an effort to rearrange the region's waters.

Chapter 4 says more about the concept just introduced, which will figure prominently in the rest of our argument—the "Growth Machine" that is set in motion by proponents of economic development. As we will note, although these proponents may devote little thought to the matter, their actions can easily end up making the landscape, and the people, far more susceptible to the effects of disaster. Again, the main roles in this part of the tale are played by canals.

Chapter 5 introduces a pair of engineering projects that proved to be critical to the fate of the city, changing the pattern of the area's waterways and thus changing the face of the city's landscape, doing so in ways that contributed to its later fate. These two projects are known by locals as the *Industrial Canal* and the *Mississippi River–Gulf Outlet.*

In essence, the city of New Orleans has long been protected by two encircling lines of defense. Chapter 6 turns to the inner ring, the system of engineered levees and floodwalls that failed so spectacularly in the time of Katrina. Next, Chapter 7 turns to the outer ring of defense, the wetlands and other natural buffers that also helped to protect New Orleans from the rages of the sea. As the chapter will spell out, it is now quite evident that the rearranging of the natural landscape by the Growth Machine was in large part responsible for the failures in that broader ring of defense. With this as background, Chapter 8 then offers a closer examination of the Mississippi River–Gulf Outlet, or MRGO. This canal is sometimes referred to in and around New Orleans as "Mr. Go," and sometimes as "the hurricane highway." It is the most prominent—and in the clarity of hindsight, perhaps the most dangerous—of all the projects ever imposed upon New Orleans by the Growth Machine.

Chapter 9 broadens the inquiry by reconsidering the widely shared temptation to treat the lessons of Katrina as being limited to New Orleans itself. This chapter takes a brief look at patterns of growth in two regions that seem utterly unlike southern Louisiana—one in California and one in Missouri. In both regions, recent "economic development" projects prove to be so familiar in their outlines that they almost look as though they were deliberately staged to re-create the story of Katrina and New Orleans. In a world where the Growth Machine is so actively and so obliviously at work, there is a deadly warning to be found in the likeness. As closing chapters normally do, finally, Chapter 10 discusses the lessons that are still to be learned from Katrina.

As will become clear, the full story of Katrina includes not just the power of the storm and the details of the location, but also the ways in which we humans had modified that location—generally doing so in ways that worsened the ultimate harm, not just to nature, but also to ourselves. The causes of that damage had to do not just with the ways in which we allowed our hardware to shape the landscape, but also the ways in which we have allowed our pursuit of economic development to shape our thinking. The consequences, unfortunately, did as well.

Those consequences ultimately came back to haunt the people of New Orleans. If we are paying attention, though, they should also haunt the rest of us. Yet they should also do more. They should direct our attention toward new ways of dealing with nature—not just in New Orleans, but everywhere—in the future. It is now too late, after all, to turn back the clock to the time before Katrina stuck. With each day that passes, however, we are making choices about the hazards that we will face in the future, and we are affecting as well the options that will be available for facing them. It is thus to shaping the future, as well as learning from the past, that this book is devoted.

Chapter 1

A Mighty Storm
Hits the Shore

W E NOTED in the prologue that Katrina became an event in human history when it left the waters of the Gulf and began to hammer the land, affecting areas that had been both settled and shaped by people. The largest concentration of population in the region, of course, is to be found in New Orleans, and for the people who lived there in 2005, the term "Katrina" has come to refer to a reality that has little to do with storm systems forming out at sea or winds spiraling at terrifying speeds as they slammed into the coast.

In the aftermath of Katrina, any number of commentaries treated the destruction of New Orleans as a more or less inevitable consequence of the city's location—very close to sea level, along a stretch of coastline that is no stranger to hurricanes. According to one local account, 172 hurricanes have affected coastal Louisiana since 1559, and 38 of them have reached New Orleans. Katrina would be by far the most expensive of them—in fact, it would become the most expensive natural disaster in the history of the United States—but it was not quite the deadliest, even for hurricanes along the U.S. Gulf Coast. That distinction is reserved for a storm that struck just over a century earlier.[1]

Columbus, of course, made his first journey in 1492, but even four hundred years later, only a few of the communities of the Gulf Coast had populations of more than a thousand souls. One of the largest was Cheniere Caminada, a thriving coastal fishing community 50 miles south of New Orleans, which by 1892 had become home to about 1500 citizens. By the next year, 1893, it would have less than half as many survivors. The other half lost their lives in a hurricane that not only destroyed their community but killed well over a thousand people in southern Louisiana. Just seven years later, an even deadlier hurricane would overwhelm what was at the time the largest of all cities along the Gulf—larger than nearby Houston—Galveston, Texas. The hapless citizens of that then-major city were not just surprised by a hurricane, but also helplessly unable to evacuate because they were living on an island. That storm set the all-time record for an American natural disaster, killing 6,000 people in Galveston alone, along with 2,000 more victims in the surrounding region.[2]

Even a few miles of separation from the nearest salt water could have provided the unfortunate residents of Galveston with substantial protection from hurricanes. Part of the reason is that, although we tend to measure a hurricane's "strength" in terms of its wind speeds, most of the actual death and destruction from a hurricane comes instead from water, in the form of storm surges. A hurricane's winds push the water in front of the storm, and, as the storm nears shore, the water builds up even higher, much as snow piles up in front of a snow shovel. Even in a region where the surface of the land is almost as flat as the surface of a calm ocean, an inland location can derive a significant level of protection from the land that lies between that location and the sea, acting as a giant shock absorber against storm surges.

As we will discuss in the next chapter, however, New Orleans is one of those inland locations.

After the two killer storms of 1893 and 1900, the residents of Louisiana showed little inclination to move back to the edge of the salt water. By the 1980s, one analysis found that only about 12 percent of the Louisiana coastline could be accessed even by rudimentary roads, while comparable figures for California and Florida were 90 percent and 74 percent, respectively.[3]

For most of southeastern Louisiana and the Mississippi Gulf

Coast, Hurricane Katrina was a significant natural disaster. In southern portions of the jurisdiction that straddles the bottom 60 miles or so of the Mississippi River, namely Plaquemines Parish (a parish being the equivalent of a county in most other states) the storm surge was roughly 20 feet high, overtopping Mississippi River levees, destroying entire communities, stripping many buildings down to dirt and concrete slabs, and leading local authorities to declare martial law. A few weeks after the storm, three of the authors of this book drove a local official back to Plaquemines Parish, where she had lived for all of her life, and where she was able to identify the likely inhabitant of a casket that had been incongruously carried away from its resting place and into the middle of a marsh, simply by the markings on the outside of the casket. The damage to the landscape, on the other hand, was so substantial that, in many areas, she had difficulty orienting herself and identifying once-familiar landmarks from the few shreds that remained.

In Mississippi, most of the state's coast was battered by the hurricane's powerful northeast quadrant, where the right hook of Katrina's counterclockwise rotation produced a huge storm surge and severe levels of physical damage as the storm came ashore. CBS News quoted state officials as estimating that 90 percent of the structures within half of a mile of the coastline were swept off their foundations and demolished. In a cruel irony, the town of Waveland would be swamped by a storm surge that some would later speculate to have been as much as 40 feet high. An official count would later report that Katrina destroyed 68,729 homes in the state.[4]

All told, Katrina-related federal disaster declarations covered 90,000 square miles, or an area nearly the size of the United Kingdom. Much of the coastal zone to the north and east of New Orleans—from Slidell, Louisiana, through all of Mississippi, and stretching into the Mobile Bay area of Alabama—was also heavily damaged. The storm killed 238 people in Mississippi alone, leaving roughly 3 million people without electricity. Katrina, in short, would be remembered as a significant natural disaster under any circumstances. Unfortunately, it was also accompanied by other disasters that were even more dramatic, particularly in and around the city of New Orleans.

Any hurricane can produce terrifying conditions. The winds roar, blowing so fiercely that large and ordinarily stationary objects—billboards, roofs, trucks, and more—can turn into deadly missiles. Water is everywhere, not just falling from the skies and driving painfully with the wind, but, even worse, rising from the seas, creating such chaos and destruction that even the most hardened of observers are often stunned by the storm's deadly power. Even by hurricane standards, however, Katrina was different. As Americans watched the mounting misery on their televisions, the customary missions of relief and rescue went nowhere. The failure of the levees was stunning enough. What was more disturbing was the fact that the "organized emergency response" of the federal government, as one Louisiana resident put it, "was none of the three."

By the time the eye of the hurricane was passing to the east of New Orleans, at roughly 9:00 a.m. on August 29, the city's physical protection structures had begun to fail—some catastrophically. Over the next several days, the organizational responses would show even greater failures. The flawed defense system—both in terms of its physical and of its human and organizational components—created enough of an "un-natural" catastrophe to qualify as a disaster in its own right, in some ways just as stunning as the physical destructiveness of the storm itself.

At least until Katrina struck, however, it seemed as though residents of the region were about as well-prepared for the onslaught as might be hoped. Experts and officials were watching carefully as Katrina churned across the Gulf, particularly when projections began to indicate that the storm was headed directly toward New Orleans. The National Weather Service broadcast an ever-rising crescendo of alarms, warning that "devastating damage" was expected not only to private homes and industrial structures, but to all living things. "At least one-half of well-constructed homes will have roof and wall failure," said one warning. Soon thereafter, another cautioned that "the majority of industrial buildings will become non-functional," that "all wood-framed low-rising apartment buildings will be destroyed," and that "high-rise office and apartment buildings will sway dangerously," some of them "to the point of total collapse. All windows will blow out."[5]

New Orleans Mayor Ray Nagin would later come under heavy criticism, but as the hurricane came over the horizon, he did encourage residents to evacuate, and on August 28, the day before Katrina struck, he issued the first mandatory evacuation order in the long history of that storm-seasoned city. In her turn, Louisiana Governor Kathleen Blanco arranged for regional roads to absorb that massive evacuation, reversing the flow for normally in-bound lanes of interstate highways. She joined in urging people to leave the city, later adding unmistakable emphasis by suggesting that those who refused to evacuate should write their social security numbers on their arms with indelible ink.

The initial encouragement and later mandatory order to leave persuaded many thousands of residents to escape before Katrina made its dramatic arrival on the scene. This was, in fact, the most successful rapid evacuation of a major city in human history—a fact that is easily overlooked in the context of a time when so much was going wrong for so many.

Disasters have a way of appearing to seek out the most vulnerable people in their paths, although that clearly says more about the vulnerabilities of those located in harm's way than it does about any motives one might be tempted to attribute to disasters. In New Orleans, the least-imperiled residents were those who were equipped with functioning automobiles, credit cards, experience of the road, and networks of friends elsewhere; the greatest dangers were reserved for those without transportation or other resources, those who had to care for ill or elderly kin, and those with the least experience of the world outside of the area. On first impressions, such a pattern can almost seem to be a grim kind of joke that disasters have a way of playing on the poor—although that is one of the reasons why it is important to seek more than just first impressions.

Still, while many of those who remained behind had little choice in the matter, many others reasoned that they could ride out the hurricane in their own homes. It is another easily overlooked fact that those people were, for the most part, quite right in their calculations. No one ever asked them to evacuate on the grounds that the levees and floodwalls were about to fail, and those who concluded that they could withstand the storm were essentially correct in their thinking.

Unfortunately, they were struck low by events that had not been fore-told in even the most desperate of warnings.

On the early morning of August 29, when Katrina first crashed ashore some miles from New Orleans itself, on-scene television reporters began to appear on the nation's screens. Most of them were enacting a now-familiar role—braced against the wind, trench coats flapping, hair twisting into snarls, shouting into hand-held microphones that the storm looked mean out here.

The winds, of course, were gusty enough to provide the familiar backdrop, but the news the reporters were broadcasting throughout that day and well into the next was implausibly good. To repeat an expression heard often that day, New Orleans looked as though it had "dodged another bullet." The storm that had battered so much of the Louisiana and Mississippi coastline was seemingly bypassing the city itself. The U.S. Army Corps of Engineers—often referred to simply as "the Corps"—issued what quickly proved to be a premature and embarrassing assessment, saying that the fact that Katrina had not caused more damage was "a testament to the structural integrity of the hurricane levee protection system."[6]

And so, for a while, it seemed. A few city blocks east of the location where the reporters were being tousled by the winds of Katrina, though, floodwaters had already begun to surge over the floodwalls along the canals that slice through the city at such peculiar angles. And as the eye of the storm veered just to the east of New Orleans, other protective structures were beginning to fail completely.

—

Days earlier, while Katrina was still in the Gulf, bearing down on New Orleans, the disaster manager of adjacent Jefferson Parish, Walter Maestri, got a personal phone call from Max Mayfield of the National Hurricane Center: "Walter, get ready, this could be the one." In many senses, Maestri had been "ready" even before he got the call. His preparedness included his participation in an earlier exercise, commissioned by the Federal Emergency Management Agency (FEMA), which had focused on a hypothetical "Hurricane Pam." Emergency managers in that exercise had concluded that a direct hit to New Orleans could create massive flooding, killing tens of thousands of people, and potentially leaving the entire New Orleans metropolitan region paralyzed for months. Maestri even had 10,000 body bags in his parish, ready for a grim duty.*

What neither he nor almost anyone else could have been ready for was the stunning absence of a federal response. What made the subsequent suffering even worse was the fact that, in a country as rich and technologically advanced as the United States—able to deliver astonishing quantities of food and medical supplies, seemingly within a matter of hours, to almost any location on earth—the help somehow failed to arrive within our own borders, day after day, even as the agony continued to grow. As the nation watched the live television coverage of the unfolding tragedy, attention turned to this second set of failures—involving not just the physical floodwalls, but the relevant "emergency response" organizations as well. In the case of the levees and floodwalls, a relatively small number of failures were sufficient to drown most of the city, just as a single hole can be enough to sink a ship. Even the Corps of Engineers would later admit that its protection system failed to function "as a system." The failures of the human and organizational emergency responses, by contrast, were stunningly systematic, involving all levels of government.

In fairness, there were also some noteworthy exceptions to the general pattern—responses that were effective and even heroic. As has been pointed out by analysts who are thoroughly familiar with disasters and emergency management, however, the most effective responses often come from ordinary citizens whose primary job responsibilities do *not* include "disaster preparedness." As has happened so often in the past, even some of the most destitute and distressed citizens of New Orleans performed remarkable acts of civic heroism, providing spontaneous help to their fellow citizens.[7]

Particularly in light of media reports of racism in predominantly white areas of rural Louisiana, it is also worth noting that untold hundreds of rural white Louisianans came to New Orleans almost

---

*Ironically, the hypothetical storm was named Pam because planners expected that named storms in a given year would never go so far into the alphabet as P. In fact, with the exception of the letters Q and X (which have never been used), the 2005 season used up all of the letters of the alphabet and more, ultimately including five characters from the Greek alphabet.

immediately, simply to help. They managed to get their boats to the city even before dawn on August 30—some four days before the National Guard appeared on the scene. With no military chain of command, they were simply offering spontaneous, humanitarian responses to a politician's request, bringing their own hunting and fishing boats to help rescue survivors, in an operation that came to be known locally as "the Cajun Flotilla." These ordinary citizens even had the presence of mind to reserve two open lanes of freeway for emergency vehicles—although some of them later noted that no such vehicles appeared during the entire time that they were engaged in rescue operations themselves. Instead, when they did see an official presence, it came two full days later, on the morning of September 1—at which time police officers managed to accomplish little except to prevent the helpful citizens from continuing their rescue efforts.

In fairness to those police officers, they apparently believed the reports of nearly unimaginable social chaos that were by then becoming widespread. As has usually been the case with disasters, however, more careful assessments would later make it clear that most of those initial, horrifying reports were almost completely unrelated to reality.[8]

Despite widespread reports of anarchy, moreover, the much-maligned citizens who were caught in the Superdome and the Convention Center—the majority of them poor and black—also managed to be much more resourceful than was commonly recognized at the time. One particularly gripping firsthand account was posted online by Larry Bradshaw and Lorrie Beth Slonsky, a pair of paramedics from California who happened to be attending a convention in New Orleans when the hurricane hit, and who argued that the real heroes of the relief effort were the ordinary working people of New Orleans.

Bradshaw and Slonsky noted that those who were fortunate enough to be able to make cell phone contact with persons outside of the city "were repeatedly told that all sorts of resources including the National Guard and scores of buses were pouring into the city." Unfortunately, "the buses and the other resources must have been invisible." When it became obvious that no buses were arriving, some of the stranded citizens decided to pool their resources and to charter buses at their own expense—only to have the buses commandeered on

The "Cajun Flotilla," early morning, August 30, 2005, as recorded by one of those heroes who participated in the rescue effort. Note that two right lanes were left "free" for emergency vehicles. Photograph by Nathan Bassiouni.

their way to New Orleans. With food and water supplies running out and with no sign of the promised evacuation, several hundred people set up camp outside the police command center, where they would be plainly visible to the media. As Bradshaw and Slonsky put it,

> In short order, the police commander came across the street to address our group. He told us he had a solution: we should walk to the Pontchartrain Expressway and cross the greater New Orleans bridge where the police had buses lined up to take us out of the city. The crowd cheered and began to move. We called everyone back and explained to the commander that there had been lots of misinformation and wrong information and was he sure that there were buses waiting for us. The commander turned to the crowd and stated emphatically, "I swear to you that the buses are there." [9]

Like so many other promises to the people of New Orleans, this one proved to be a lie—but this was a lie with a particularly ironic twist. There was indeed a police presence on the other side of the bridge, but it was provided by armed sheriff's deputies from the predominantly white suburb of Gretna, who fired live ammunition over the heads of the group of unarmed survivors, cursing at them and telling them there would be no way that Gretna's finest would allow "the problems of New Orleans" to come across the river.

Still, the story did not stop there:

> All day long, we saw other families, individuals, and groups make the same trip up the incline in an attempt to cross the bridge, only to be turned away. Some [were] chased away with gunfire, others simply told no, others . . . verbally berated and humiliated. Thousands of New Orleaners were prevented and prohibited from self-evacuating the city on foot. Meanwhile, the only two city shelters sank further into squalor and disrepair. The only way across the bridge was by vehicle. We saw workers stealing trucks, buses, moving vans, semi-trucks, and any car that could be hot-wired. All were packed with people trying to escape the misery New Orleans had become.
>
> Our little encampment began to blossom. Someone stole a water delivery truck and brought it up to us. Let's hear it for looting! A mile or so down the freeway, an army truck lost a couple of pallets of C-rations on a tight turn. We ferried the food back to our camp in shopping carts. Now secure with the two necessities, food and water; cooperation, community, and creativity flowered. We organized a cleanup and hung garbage bags from the rebar poles. We made beds from wood pallets and cardboard. We designated a storm drain as the bathroom and the kids built an elaborate enclosure for privacy out of plastic, broken umbrellas, and other scraps. We even organized a food recycling system where individuals could swap out parts of C-rations (applesauce for babies and candies for kids!).
>
> This was a process we saw repeatedly in the aftermath of Katrina. When individuals had to fight to find food or water, it meant looking out for yourself only. You had to do whatever it took to find water for your kids or food for your parents. When these basic needs were met, people began to look out for each other, working together and constructing a community. If the relief organizations had saturated the city with food and water in the first two or three days, the desperation, the frustration, and the ugliness would not have set in.

The following day, another group of the predominantly poor and black citizens managed to outsmart the police officials who were there to "serve and protect" them. They had heard about the incidents on the Gretna Bridge, but they decided that continuing to wait for the promised arrival of help was no longer an option. As they pondered their predicament, they happened to notice the many trucks that were still parked at the facilities of the local bottled water supplier, Kentwood Springs, several blocks away—an observation that quickly led to a plan. If there were any vehicle that the police would not stop, they reasoned, it would be a water truck—and with their large wheels, the trucks would be able to get through floodwaters that were still several feet deep. A small crowd of determined survivors waded through the floodwaters, got to the trucks, figured out how to hot-wire the ones that were still working, pulled out almost all of the bottles of water, and hid their fellow human beings where cargoes of water were normally stored. The trucks managed to deliver their human cargoes to safety, across the Sunshine Bridge, many miles from the Superdome—arriving just ahead of some of the chartered buses that finally managed to make more or less the same trip.

Even one of the agencies within the Homeland Security Department—the U.S. Coast Guard—should be singled out for its effective emergency response. The Coast Guard moved helicopters and other vulnerable equipment out of the way as the hurricane approached, but then moved in quickly afterward, joining the Cajun Flotilla in making hundreds to thousands of rescues, and delivering badly needed help. There might be an important lesson in the exceptional performance of the Coast Guard: being an agency that often needs to save people who are caught in violent weather, the Coast Guard learned long ago to rescue people first and ask for permission later.[10]

Elsewhere in the Homeland Security Department, however, the Federal Emergency Management Agency (FEMA) concentrated primarily on waiting for orders. It was a strange, nearly paralyzed pattern of behavior from an agency that, after all, was supposed to be in charge of "emergency *management*," not just emergency observation.

Before Katrina, the last time most Americans had paid much attention to FEMA had been in the aftermath of Hurricane Andrew in 1992, when the agency was widely faulted for having performed badly, perhaps in part because it was headed by political associates of the first President Bush rather than by disaster professionals. During the eight years of the Clinton administration, FEMA was widely

Water truck that helped survivors to escape from New Orleans to the Sunshine Bridge. Note that water bottles were removed to make room for human cargo. Photograph by Nathan Bassiouni.

seen as having improved dramatically, thanks to professional leadership. Unfortunately, the agency lost most of its top professional leaders, as well as most of its political priority, under the second Bush administration. Things got significantly worse after the attacks of September 11, 2001, when a heightened emphasis on terrorism led FEMA and a number of other agencies to be thrown into the bureaucratic stewpot called the Department of Homeland Security, which would be filled with confusion for many years to come. The erosion of FEMA's priority under the two Presidents Bush was ironic: it was none other than Senator Prescott Bush, of Connecticut—father of the first President Bush, grandfather of the second—who had been the driving force behind the Bush Hurricane Survey Act of 1955, which responded to the rare experience of a hurricane reaching Connecticut by instructing the Corps of Engineers to fortify the Atlantic and Gulf coasts of the U.S. against hurricanes.[11]

Unfortunately, during the pressing time of need in the wake of Katrina, the top officials of FEMA and Homeland Security seemed to be some of the few people in America who were unaware that tens of thousands of New Orleanians were in desperate need, waiting exactly where they had been told to wait for help. Enrico Quarantelli—possibly the most senior figure in the entire field of disaster management—called Katrina "the worst mishandled disaster I have ever seen in my life, and I have been studying disasters since 1949."[12]

The National Science Foundation's Independent Levee Investigation Team was probably striving for scrupulous fairness when it described FEMA as having been "organized for failure." The reality may have been even worse.

The lone FEMA employee in the New Orleans Superdome, a career professional named Marty Bahamonde, was sending increasingly frantic e-mail messages to his superiors in Washington. One of them, on August 31, warned superiors of a situation that had gone "past critical," adding that many people would "die within hours." As noted in an Associated Press report, however, less than three hours after that message, the press secretary for FEMA's director, Mike Brown, wrote colleagues to complain that the director needed more time that evening to finish his dinner at a Baton Rouge restaurant.[13]

Another example of the federal government's ineffective responses to Katrina involves the USS *Bataan*, a large ship designed for Marine amphibious assaults, which happened to be in the Gulf of Mexico during the hurricane. The ship—complete with its own helicopters, doctors, hospital facilities, operating rooms, and beds for six hundred patients, as well as the capacity to make up to 100,000 gallons/day of its own potable water—began heading toward New Orleans after the hurricane passed. The *Bataan* even dispatched a 135-foot-long landing craft, the LCU-1656, with a crew of sixteen, including a doctor, plus enough food, water, and fuel to remain self-sufficient for ten days. The LCU-1656 was within forty miles of New Orleans when it was ordered to turn around, without delivering its cargo, because the *Bataan* had been ordered to move to the waters off Biloxi, Mississippi.[14]

The citizens of New Orleans, meanwhile, were subjected to ever-increasing torment. An unknown but large number of them died while waiting for the kinds of help that could have saved their lives.

Days earlier, as the storm was approaching, New Orleans mayor

Nagin had announced that the Superdome would be open as a shelter of last resort, and by Sunday evening, just a few hours before Katrina would strike, city officials estimated that some 9,000 people had already showed up to avail themselves of that "last resort." To its credit, and in contrast to the spectacular failures that followed the actual arrival of the hurricane, FEMA had shown at least some signs of sensible preparation, having sent seven semi-trailers full of food and water to that location—enough to supply two days of food for twice that many people and three days' worth of water for three times that many.

At the time, those supplies probably seemed sufficient. After the Hurricane Pam exercise, FEMA officials had told local authorities that the locals might have to be on their own for 48 or even 60 hours after a real storm, but that a massive federal response could be expected to take care of the region's needs after that. The director of Homeland Security for New Orleans, Terry Ebbert, told the *Washington Post* that the city's plan was to "hang in there for 48 hours and wait for the cavalry." The previously mentioned disaster manager for neighboring Jefferson Parish, Walter Maestri, similarly expected the cavalry to arrive as promised. "Like a fool," he later noted, "I believed them." Maestri had participated in a series of conference calls on Sunday, August 28; by the time of the last call, around midnight, he was specifically asking for medical units, mortuary units, ice, water, power, and National Guard troops. "We laid it all out," he told the *Post.* "And then we sat here for five days waiting. Nothing!"[15]

"Nothing but misery" might have been a more apt description. As the water poured into the city, more citizens poured into the Superdome—an estimated 20,000 of them, all bringing along their own private miseries and then experiencing the collective ones, all compounded by the intense heat and humidity. By Monday night, Governor Blanco had contacted President Bush—then some four weeks into a five-week vacation at his ranch in Crawford, Texas— telling him that Louisiana urgently needed his help. "We need everything you've got," she said. The state still needed the help the next day, and the day after that.

On Tuesday, August 30, Michael Chertoff—the secretary of the Department of Homeland Security, of which FEMA had become one relatively small part—declared the unfolding disaster to be an "incident of national significance," which at least theoretically signaled a heightened level of response from the federal government's new post-9/11 system. Unfortunately, he did not actually bother to announce this "incident of national significance" in public until the next day. By then—Wednesday, August 31—an additional 25,000 evacuees had gathered in the New Orleans Convention Center, many of them having been unable to get to the flooded area around the Superdome, and most of them having become increasingly desperate as food and water supplies dwindled and disappeared.

Officials from the U.S. military's Northern Command finally started sending army brigade commanders and their staffs to the region on the next day, Thursday, September 1, but despite the fact that the military had access to many of the very supplies that disaster managers knew from experience to be needed—water, food, medicines, and the kinds of mobile communication systems that tend to be equally useful on a foreign battlefield or a domestic disaster zone where telephone service had been wiped out—the only request the U.S. military received from FEMA was for half a dozen helicopters.

The National Guard units that finally did manage to straggle into the city, meanwhile, were not exactly well equipped. Guard officials in Louisiana and Mississippi evidently had no contingency plans to handle the disruption of transportation and communication systems: "they had only one satellite phone for the entire Mississippi coast, because the others were in Iraq." A week after Katrina struck, two authors of this book traveled to Uptown New Orleans on a pet-rescue mission for a medical staffer who had been evacuated by helicopter from her hospital. As we were leaving on Interstate 10, we passed long columns of National Guard troops with embarrassingly dilapidated vehicles—some of World War II vintage, some towed by National Guard wreckers, and some with holes rusted right through the bodies—that were still streaming into the city. Clearly, the good stuff was in Iraq.[16]

It would not be until Friday, September 2—four full days after Katrina slammed ashore—when President Bush finally decided to end his vacation and fly over New Orleans. His presence shut down air support for the city, but it did allow him to look down on the misery. In what many saw as a striking understatement, he noted that his government's performance was "not acceptable." What he evidently did find acceptable, on the other hand, was the performance of Michael Brown, the head of FEMA—a man whose main qualifications for the job, aside from his personal and political connections, was that he may have served previously as an official of an Arabian horse association. As the president put it, in what quickly became a famous phrase of praise, "Brownie, you're doing a heck of a job."

"Brownie" and his agency, unfortunately, may not have been the only ones doing "a heck of a job." Others had been hard at work much earlier, and their actions may have contributed to the drowning of New Orleans in the first place.

Many of the events of that tragic week—the second, human story of Katrina—will seem painfully familiar, even years later. Much of the drama of that week, after all, unfolded on television screens across the country and around the world. As noted in the prologue of this book, however, the stage was set for that drama by a third and much earlier story—one that had started decades or even centuries earlier, almost as soon as Europeans first set foot in this vicinity. In a process that gathered speed and momentum over the course of the nineteenth and especially the twentieth centuries, human forces, almost as powerful as those of nature, profoundly altered the "near-perfect situation" that nature had provided on the banks of the Mississippi River. One of the consequences—as illustrated by a pair of other powerful storms—is that Katrina might not have created nearly so much human suffering if the same storm had attacked the same stretch of coastline just forty years earlier.

Chapter 2

The Setting

NEW ORLEANS has long held a special place in America, culturally and economically, but its location in the Louisiana coastal wetlands makes it unique in a geographic sense as well. At the time when Hurricane Katrina made landfall, a third of the nation's seafood originated in Louisiana's wetlands, and the complex of ports along the Mississippi, from Baton Rouge to New Orleans, was the focal point of commerce for the nation's heartland, collectively constituting the nation's busiest port, by volume. About 20 percent of the nation's energy supply, mainly from offshore oil and gas platforms, was passing through and being supported from the Louisiana coast. Perhaps the most unusual fact about the city's setting, though, is that New Orleans is quite unlike most port cities, such as London or New York. Rather than being located on the coast, this key port for the Mississippi River is located well inland, about 120 river miles up from what is currently the river's main outlet, Southwest Pass.[1]

Part of the reason is that, unlike most of the continent's coastline, the southern edge of Louisiana is almost as much a part of the sea as it is of the land.

The fact that southern Louisiana exists at all has to do with special deliveries, over thousands of years, from thousands of miles to the north. The region owes its existence to the gradual buildup of billions of tons of silt—the gift of what, after all, we call the "muddy" Mississippi River. For millennia, the river has delivered topsoil from the regions we now know as Iowa, Tennessee, South Dakota, and beyond. In the process, all of that muddy water has built up an ever-broadening swath of wetlands along the Gulf of Mexico. The result is a vast, open region—known by geologists as an alluvial or deltaic plain—that stretches across almost 200 miles of southern Louisiana, from the Chandeleur Islands, off the coast of Mississippi, on the east, to Vermilion Bay on the west.

Filling a jar full of Mississippi water and then setting it down and watching the suspended particles settle—which they do only slowly—can offer a small-scale illustration of the process. So long as the water keeps moving, as in a shaking jar or a rolling river, the soil particles stay suspended, but when the motion stops, they start to settle. The process is particularly notable where the flowing river waters run into a sea-level obstacle that is not about to be shoved aside. There, along the sea-level boundary, where the river's momentum has been stopped by the Gulf of Mexico, the Mississippi has deposited countless layers of silt, spreading them across the landscape and contributing to the slow, muddy creation of new land.[2]

The southern edge of Louisiana has long been a fluid environment, both literally and figuratively. Radiating across the landscape, and shifting constantly, are multiple rivers, bayous, and distributaries—the last-named being channels that flow out of the main current of the river, "distributing" the water as they spread. As one mouth of the river would gradually choke with sediment, creating an impediment for the waters upstream, the river would carve other channels, then others and still others, in a "braided" pattern. Historically, most of the flow was split between numerous dividing and rejoining channels, with few of those channels ever carrying more than 20 percent of the total flow of the ancient river.

The Mississippi has been a patient but persistent builder, generally working at rates of just a fraction of an inch at a time. Through constantly shifting deposition, channelization, and erosion, the river has been engaged for thousands and thousands of years in building up a series of what geologists call "deltaic lobes" across all of what is now southeastern Louisiana.

In addition to the building of deltas, the many paths of the river have created land in another way. In most parts of the globe, water seems to obey the law of gravity, carving the kinds of valleys where the rivers themselves occupy the lowest locations, where the lowest land is immediately adjacent, and where flowing water continues to work on the business of carving the valley bottoms still deeper. In deltaic plains like southeastern Louisiana, however, it may seem to the visitor almost as if that aspect of the law of gravity has been inverted. The land initially appears to be flat, but closer examination reveals that the "high" ground is next to where rivers now flow, or where they did in the past, with land levels getting gradually lower across the areas that are farther away from current or past river channels.

The basic reason again involves what happens when muddy waters slow down—in this case, when rivers and streams overflow their banks. Because the water that overflows the banks is moving more slowly than the river's primary current, the flooding water will no longer carry the full load of soil being conveyed by the roiling, more rapidly moving water in the main current, meaning that the silt and sand will soon begin to settle. The heaviest particles tend to drop the fastest, being deposited closest to the river channels, along the banks of the river. Over time, these deposits gradually build up the region's "natural levees"—stretches of elevated ground running along the banks of active rivers and bayous.

To people from other areas, bayous look like slow-moving rivers. Technically, the distinction is that the water in a bayou can reverse the direction of its flow as the tide rolls in and out, but like many other technical distinctions, this one has often been handled in a relaxed way in the naming of Louisiana's waterways. The slightly higher slivers of land along the riverbanks, on the other hand, have consistently been called "levees," ever since the French explorers first used the term *levée*—the past participle of *lever*, "to raise."

One final point that needs to be made about the land-building is that it actually involves two sets of processes, working against one another. As the region has experienced the steady deliveries of soil from the Mississippi and its tributaries, it has also experienced opposing forces—particularly erosion and the continual processes of subsidence—as those tons of deposits have been compressed under their own weight. Southern Louisiana exists only because the river has long delivered new loads of sediment slightly faster than the older ones compressed, decayed, subsided, or eroded. Over the centuries, though, this agonizingly slow process has led to a phenomenal accumulation of soil deposits, extending well into the Gulf of Mexico. In some cases, those deposits are hundreds or even thousands of feet deep, but not even the highest of them rise to more than a few feet above mean sea level.

The Mississippi still delivers to this region an average of almost half a million tons of sediment a day, but the sediment loads have changed considerably over time. Roughly half a century before Katrina, in 1951, the daily load was more than three times that high—1,576,000 tons per day. Another century before that—before farmers began plowing up the forests and prairie grasses that once covered almost the entire Mississippi River basin—a local observer from Grand Isle, on the Louisiana coast, spoke of clear water. At least during the summer, he reported, after the Mississippi's spring floods, "The beach is smooth, and covered with small white shells, the water is clear and salt." Even so, the Mississippi and its tributaries have carried enough silt down to southern Louisiana to have built up the most extensive system of coastal marshes in the United States—3.5 million acres of coastal wetlands, or about 40 percent of all of the coastal wetlands in the continental United States.[3]

According to the U.S. Geological Survey, much of the decline in sediment loads during the latter half of the twentieth century can be traced to the building of dams, particularly along the Missouri River, which reduced the Missouri's annual deliveries of sediment by 70–80 percent. The dam-building was coupled with a greatly increased effort to confine the Mississippi within a more disciplined channel by building levees along the riverbanks, particularly following the disastrous floods of 1927.

These two actions—trapping much of the sediment behind dams and keeping most of the rest bottled up in the main channels—meant that the river could no longer deliver as much new soil, nor could it spread across the landscape to add the new deposits on top of the old ones. Those former deposits, however, continued to compress under their own weight and to erode from the actions of current, tides, and storms. The changes proved to be sufficient to upset what turns out to have been an unexpectedly delicate balance, leading to the slow reversal of thousands of years of land-building.[4]

Land and Life

The net effect of the Mississippi's land-building process has been that almost all of the lands of southeastern Louisiana, literally as well as officially, are wetlands—swamps and marshes of haunting beauty and tremendous ecological vitality, but also of potential dangers and threats to humans. The huge open bays and estuaries can be treacherous in a sudden storm, and a balky motor can leave an unprepared skipper stranded, miles from the nearest road or human habitation. Except along stretches of relatively "high" ground, meanwhile, the wetlands themselves can be almost impossible to cross on foot, presenting obvious challenges to human settlement.

The wetlands, moreover, are teeming with life, but one aspect of that fact is that they are filled with what a local resident has called "things that will stick you, sting you, stab you, and bite you." Water moccasins and alligators are the most legendary of the region's potentially hostile natural inhabitants, but the environment is also nearly perfect for some of nature's most ravenous insects—mosquitoes and deer flies, to name two—both of which respond with annual population explosions into the billions. The mosquitoes attack mainly at dawn and dusk, should the traveler be foolish enough to be outside at those times, but the deer flies bite all day. Even so, humans have long chosen to travel through the wetlands, willing to overlook the insects in the name of other natural wonders, because the Louisiana coastal wetlands—rich with fish, shellfish, waterfowl, and fur-bearing mammals—constitute one of the most productive ecosystems on the planet.

Spain had claimed Florida by the early 1500s, and the land we now know as Louisiana was first officially noted by European explorers soon thereafter, within just a few years of Columbus's initial encounter with what he thought to be "India." In 1519, Alonso Álvarez de Pineda, a cartographer commissioned by Francisco de Garay, the

Spanish governor of Jamaica, traveled as far west along the coast as present-day Texas, becoming the first European to record having seen the Mississippi River, which his map called *El Rio del Espíritu Santo*—the River of the Holy Spirit. There would be little other evidence of European activity in the region for the first two centuries after the arrival of Columbus, but Europeans did affect the population density of the region's native inhabitants in one important way during that period—through the introduction of diseases. The new maladies brought by the Europeans spread through the native populations with such deadly efficiency that, when later European settlers reported vast stretches of the continent to be largely "empty," they may well have been reporting their observations with reasonable accuracy.

The Mississippi delta may have been visited by Cabeza de Vaca and the other survivors of a Spanish expedition in 1528, and it was probably seen by some of De Soto's men in 1541 or 1542, but not until 1682, 190 years after the first voyage of Columbus, would Europeans travel down the Mississippi River to its mouth. The explorers to make that first trip were led by René-Robert de LaSalle, who had been trading with natives in the Montreal region. Ironically, he was searching for the legendary "northwest passage," but when natives told him about the existence of great rivers, he listened, heading south instead. After leading a small flotilla of canoes all the way down the great river to the Gulf of Mexico, he claimed for France the territory drained by the Mississippi River and its tributaries, naming it "Louisiana" in honor of the man remembered by historians as the Sun King, Louis the Great.[5]

Well before the arrival of the Europeans, the area's native inhabitants had developed a pattern of coming to the coast to fish and hunt in the coastal wetlands from fall to spring, and then moving well away from the coast during the summers. When Europeans and their descendants began to filter into the area in the early eighteenth century, they preferred to establish fixed settlements, interrupting the fluid process of land-building and starting a somewhat less fluid process of city-building. A particularly notable example was the small settlement they established along a stretch of the natural levee of what we now call the Mississippi River.

The first European settlement in the New Orleans area was actually founded in 1708, at the headwaters of a small waterway known as Bayou St. John—well within the boundaries of the area that New Orleans would cover by the end of the twentieth century—but most historians trace the origins of New Orleans to 1718. That was when the early French governor of Louisiana, Jean-Baptiste Le Moyne de Bienville, established the city in the location that later generations would know as the Vieux Carré ("old square"), or the French Quarter. It was a location where the natural levee along the dominant channel of the Mississippi River stretched in a crescent in both directions, providing room for future expansion—and providing as well the origin of New Orleans' nickname, the "Crescent City."

The location he chose, however, had to do not just with the Mississippi River, but also with the above-noted Bayou St. John—a small stream that was little more than a drainage channel for the back or downhill side of the Mississippi's natural levee. The importance of this small bayou for the city's origins can be guessed from one of the earliest known maps of New Orleans, which actually shows more of Bayou St. John, along its upper edge, than of the Mississippi River itself.

Bayou St. John drains to the north, into "Lake" Pontchartrain, which is actually a bay of brackish water that is connected through a pair of relatively narrow passes to the Gulf of Mexico. There was already a settlement at Mobile Bay, and this location meant that ships could sail behind the barrier islands that protect what we now know as the Alabama and Mississippi coasts, reaching Lake Pontchartrain through one of the passes, the Rigolets. By sailing across Lake Pontchartrain and then up Bayou St. John, boats could reach well into what the twentieth century would consider to be the city of New Orleans, although the settlement of the early days was still so small that the end of the trip involved a portage across a short stretch of land.[6]

Bayou St. John cuts between the Metairie and Gentilly ridges, both of which are segments of a natural levee from an ancient channel of the Mississippi River. A third former levee, known today as the Esplanade Ridge, runs southeastward from Bayou St. John to the current natural levee of the Mississippi. This ridge facilitated the portage

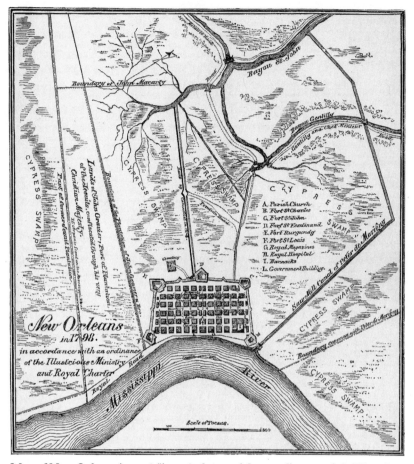

Map of New Orleans in 1798 "in accordance with an ordinance of the Illustrious Ministry and Royal Charter." Note that the map is approximately 45 degrees away from lining up with compass directions; North is toward the upper right.

between the bayou and the river, and it had been used by Native Americans long before Europeans "discovered" the region. Although there were competing sites, the geography of the Esplanade Ridge made the terminus of the portage between Bayou St. John and the river the ideal spot for the small settlement that would ultimately come to dominate the trade from the entire midsection of the North American continent.

The clever water route from the east also avoided the extended sail south from the Mississippi coast through unprotected Gulf waters to reach the treacherous bird's-foot delta at the end of the river, at the same time avoiding the battle against the flow of more than 100 miles of the lower Mississippi River to reach the same location. As noted above, this also meant that New Orleans was an inland city, protected from hurricane winds and water by a broad swath of wetlands and cypress swamps—mosquito-infested, but resource-rich and ecologically healthy.

It was just four years after the new city was officially founded that New Orleans became the capital of French Louisiana, in 1722. Still, the region would have few settlers of European ancestry until the middle and later years of the 1700s. A key part of that change took place after the 1762 Treaty of Fontainebleau and the 1763 Treaty of Paris—which ended what France and Britain remember as the Seven Years' War, or what most American schoolchildren learn to call the "French and Indian War"—when France ceded New Orleans, plus the vast area drained by the Mississippi River, to the Spanish.

In 1795, the government of the still-young United States negotiated with Spain, obtaining what was known as the "right of deposit" under what historical footnotes remember as the Pinckney treaty, permitting U.S. interests to store goods in New Orleans without paying duty before the goods were exported. Five years later, however, another secret agreement among European powers—the Treaty of San Ildefonso, signed in 1800—led to the "retrocession" of the territory to Napoléon I and thus back to France. That pact is surely one of the least well-remembered of many agreements among European powers over the centuries, but it had important consequences for the still-new nation that at that time was clinging to the eastern edge of the North American continent. Among the treaty's other implications, it would be the reason why many generations of American schoolchildren would learn that Thomas Jefferson's "Louisiana Purchase" three years later, in 1803, was an agreement not with Spain, but with France.

Jefferson was motivated in part by the fact that the French had revoked the right of deposit during the previous year, but mainly Jefferson was interested in gaining control of the city that had the potential to control or constrain the trade from the entire Mississippi

River Valley. In words that would later be emphasized by the best-known historical geography of the city, Jefferson noted, "There is on the globe one spot, the possessor of which is our natural and habitual enemy. It is New Orleans."[7]

Congress had authorized the U.S. negotiators, James Monroe and Robert Livingston, to offer up to $2 million to purchase the east bank of the Mississippi; Jefferson secretly authorized them to offer over $9 million just for New Orleans and the area known at the time as West Florida (the vaguely delineated stretch of the Gulf Coast to the east of the city). In part because France faced the prospect of renewed war with England—and in part because of the prospect that the new United States government might try to take the territory by force if he refused to sell it to them—Napoléon Bonaparte eventually offered to sell the Americans the entire Louisiana territory. Acting on their own, Monroe and Livingston agreed to a purchase price of $15 million—over $3 million of which actually came back to Americans, settling claims they had lodged against France. On December 20, 1803, after Congress had agreed to ratify the purchase as a formal treaty, the size of the United States suddenly doubled, and New Orleans became for the first time an "American" city.

Acadiana

This still-small city, and the region that surrounded it, was quickly becoming as diverse as America itself. During the Spanish period (1762–1800), and even before it, German settlers had come into the area, establishing themselves along the wide natural levees of the Mississippi north of New Orleans; the area became known as the "German Coast," and to this day, Louisiana remains home to communities with names like Des Allemands. Settlers from the Canary Islands—an archipelago of seven islands about 100 miles west of the coast of Morocco, controlled by Spain—were relocated to Louisiana to increase Spanish presence, and descendents of the original "Isleños" can still be recognized today. Families from southern Spain were similarly moved to a community about 125 miles to the west of New Orleans, along the natural levee of Bayou Teche, which is still known as New Iberia.

A visitor to that community today, however, is far less likely to hear Spanish accents than French ones, brought to the region by one of the most distinctive groups of settlers ever to move into Louisiana—or for that matter, into almost any region of the present-day United States. They were part of a diaspora that began in 1755, when the British took over control of "Arcadia," the previously French-controlled area of eastern Canada that the French by then called "Acadie" and that we know today as New Brunswick and Nova Scotia. The French-speaking exiles were dispersed to many parts of the globe, including the American colonies, England, France, and as far away as New Zealand. It was a longing to recreate their former success in the New World, however, that led many of these exiles to the formerly French Catholic colony of Louisiana, even though, by that time, the French had ceded control to the Spanish. When they moved to southern Louisiana, they were called "Arcadians"—a term that was quickly shortened to "Acadians"—and we remember them today as the ancestors of the people and culture we call "Cajun."[8]

The region, sensibly enough, is often called "Acadiana," or Cajun Louisiana, but academic analysts have pointed out that the region's culture is so thoroughly characterized by inclusiveness that the name of "Acadiana" is best understood not in ethnic terms, but as denoting the region's broader cultural ethos and distinctive ways of life. The Acadians who came to Louisiana from their former home in eastern Canada developed the core of that ethos, but many other groups have enjoyed it, and contributed to it, as well. The Acadians mixed with the pre-Cajun inhabitants of the region, including Native Americans as well as the earlier German settlers, who added the accordion and numerous food traditions to the increasingly rich mixture of Cajun culture. In the eighteenth century, French, Spanish, African, Caribbean, and Anglo-American settlers, as well as the surviving Native Americans, joined the Acadians in settling the region. In short order, the ethnic and cultural mix of the region's inhabitants proved to be as rich as its famous gumbo.

At a time when entire regions of the world have sunk into ethnic violence, coastal Louisiana offers a lesson for successful ethnic and cultural coexistence that deserves much closer attention. For those who wish to learn from this admirable example, one key point is that the environmental richness and the cultural richness do not seem to exist in isolation from each other. The individuals who have built communities, raised their families, and earned their living along the coast of Louisiana have a deeply rooted connection to place, interwoven with and dependent upon the rich natural resources of the wetlands. Part of the reason that the region could be home to such a richness of cultural diversity, in other words, is that southern Louisiana is also home to one of the richest concentrations of natural resources on the planet. Those resources have long provided the kinds of ecological vitality and variety that could support an unusually broad assortment of occupations. Each population, in turn, made its own distinctive cultural contributions to the region, including new techniques for utilizing natural resources and drawing sustenance from the natural wealth of the Louisiana coast.[9]

The earlier migrations were followed by Haitians, Italians, Irish, Chinese, Filipinos, Croatians, and most recently, Vietnamese, with each group bringing new ideas. The Croatians, for example, were the ones who helped develop Louisiana's oyster industry. Major influxes of Italians into New Orleans and the wetlands added further to the cuisine as well as the cultural mix. Chinese immigrants brought the technique of drying shrimp—an innovation that would for the first time permit shrimp transportation from the wetland communities to New Orleans and that, until the introduction of commercial ice production much later, would remain the only way to preserve the shrimp for shipping. Over time, the cultural mix also came to include sugar processing methods from the West Indies, architecture and construction techniques from Spain and Haiti, land tenure and mapping from France, and vegetable cultivation, food preparation, and music from nearly every continent on earth.[10]

Even in terms of black-white relationships, the region's residents got along with one another in more amicable ways than were common at the time in the American South. In the early years of European settlement, during the eighteenth century, escaped slaves, known by the Spanish term *cimarrones*, were able to establish their own communities within the security of the marsh. Over time—perhaps in part because the New Orleans region was settled by people from so many cultures, living in close proximity to one another—it was powerfully influenced by cultures of the Caribbean and port cities around the world, including a value system of equality and the opportunity to buy one's freedom. In addition, although African Americans were enslaved on some of the French, Spanish, and later "American" plantations, few Cajun farm owners held slaves.

The African American population increased with the 1803 Louisiana Purchase, as American farmers from the Tennessee, Alabama, and Mississippi territories bought the higher land along the bayous and used slaves to work sugar plantations. The end of the Civil War, however, brought about not just the abolition of slavery, but the imposition of sharper racial separatism. Still, African Americans continued their involvement in agriculture, especially in growing sugar cane, and thus they did not frequently migrate away from the drained agricultural lands. The region's surviving Native Americans, on the other hand, were scattered throughout the emerging agricultural lands and later were pushed out of the area, often moving south and into more permanent settlements, rather than the more seasonal ones they had formed in the past, and relying on fishing and trapping to sustain a living.[11]

Because New Orleans was the first major settlement in the region to be populated by people of European descent, early European settlement of southeastern Louisiana radiated out from there. The patterns included more fixed settlements than had been the case among Native Americans, but the newcomers who survived in this bountiful but challenging landscape for more than a few years quickly learned to pay attention to the fact that, as the Native Americans had long known, the low-lying regions of Louisiana were prone to frequent flooding. Following the sensible example of the region's Native inhabitants, the Europeans thus generally built their homes on what passes in the region as "high ground," settling in "string towns" that stretched out for many miles along the natural levees, establishing settlement patterns that continue to the present.

It was not until more than 300 years after the first voyage of Columbus—following the Louisiana Purchase of 1803, and several decades after the arrival of the Cajuns—that English-speaking settlers became more common. Continuing to emulate the example of the Native Americans and the Cajuns who had come to the region before them, these new settlers also clung mainly to the natural levees—not just those of the Mississippi River, but also those of earlier channels and distributaries, including Bayou Lafourche, the Atchafalaya River, and Bayou Teche. Settlement also moved into the coastal wetlands, again taking place on the remains of natural levees, but also on embedded fragments of ancient coastlines (called chenieres, after the French word for the oak trees, *chênes*, that grew on the higher ground) and barrier islands. By the mid-1800s, there were over 100 settlements in the wetlands of the deltaic plain alone, most of which depended for their livelihoods on harvesting natural resources.[12]

As the population of the region continued to grow, the Cajuns, too, eventually moved to more isolated areas, which also happened to be some of the more productive marshes and swamps, where the abundance of alligators, oysters, shrimp, fish, and fur-bearing mammals allowed them to live off the natural bounty of Louisiana's wetlands. Despite legal, social, and economic pressures to conform to the cultural models introduced by the "new Americans," the Cajun communities continued to maintain their French language and traditional, European-based customs. In some areas, French remained the primary language for the elderly population into the 1970s, and the distinctive melodies of Cajun speech can still be heard today, particularly in smaller communities. More broadly, Cajun music, cuisine, and *joie de vivre* (joy of living) continue not just to reflect the natural productivity of coastal Louisiana but to add to the cultural richness of the region.[13]

Chapter 3

Slicing Through
the Swamps

NY REFERENCE to the rich cultural stew that is southern Louisiana would be incomplete without taking
note of the liquid in that stew. As folklorist Nicholas Spitzer points out, understanding southern Louisiana requires
a deep knowledge of human relationships with water—specifically
including the rich natural resources that can be found in a land that
is "saturated," not just in the sense of cultural diversity, but also literally. Particularly during the past few centuries, though, humans have
done much to rearrange those saturated soils.[1]

One of the first ways in which local leaders began to alter the
region's natural environment was to extend the modest waterway
noted in the previous chapter, Bayou St. John, by digging the small
canal shown on early maps, to bring waterborne commerce farther
into the heart of the city, and naming it the Carondelet Canal, in
honor of the man who initiated it, Louisiana governor Francisco Luis
Hector, Baron de Carondelet. This project, also later known as the
"old Basin Canal," was completed in 1794, near the end of the period
when Spain controlled Louisiana (1762–1800). The canal connected
Bayou St. John to what at the time was the back of the city, near
America's oldest African American neighborhood, known as Treme.

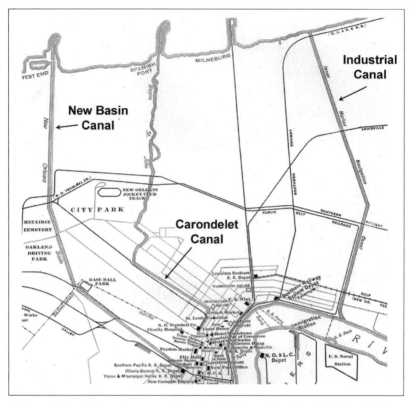

A map of New Orleans from 1921, showing the Carondelet, New Basin, and Industrial Canals. Note that even 200 years after the city's founding, most development was still concentrated along the relatively high ground, close to the Mississippi River.

A 1921 map is one of the few we have ever found that shows the locations of the Carondelet Canal, plus the later New Basin Canal and the much later Industrial Canal. Note from the location of the streets at that time, more than 200 years after the founding of the city, that there was still no indication that the lower and more marshy land, farther away from the Mississippi, would come to be filled in by urban development in the decades to follow.

The beginning of the city's first important canal could scarcely have been considered auspicious. Initially dug by prisoners and slaves, the Carondelet Canal was only about a mile and a half long, and it appears to have been intended as much to improve drainage as to increase waterborne commerce. Shallow, and infested by the tough roots of the region's native cypress trees, it was initially hard to navigate. In addition, Governor Carondelet was transferred in 1797, just three years after the completion of the canal. By the time of the American takeover of the city in 1803, the canal had already fallen into disrepair.

After the Louisiana Purchase, James Pitot and the Orleans Navigation Company worked hard to improve the canal, which was widened and deepened several times. Most of the trade on the canal, however, continued to have little to do with life on the Mississippi River. Instead, the focus was on meeting the growing needs of a still-small settlement that was only starting to turn into a city. Sailing vessels brought oysters, charcoal, and a broad assortment of other goods. Particularly important were lumber and other building materials from the North Shore of Lake Pontchartrain, as well as from the swamps between the existing city and the lake. Within ten years of the Louisiana Purchase in 1803, the canal was "of great advantage to the city, particularly as the products of the lake and back country, such as fish, lime, tar, pitch, and various other articles, find an easy water access to the inhabitants." Within another ten years, the canal had become a major commercial route between New Orleans and points to the north and east.[2]

The canal also became the site for other kinds of development. It got its unofficial name of the "Old Basin Canal" from the fact that there was a "turning basin" at the terminus or end of the canal, some 80,000 square feet in area, where vessels could turn around, reversing course. For comparison purposes, the total floor area of today's Superdome in New Orleans is a bit more than three times that large—269,000 square feet.

The basin, which was also used as a landing depot, was the hub of commercial activity. Writing in 1822, John Adems Paxton reported that "We frequently see in the Basin from 70 to 80 sail [boats], of from 550 to 600 barrels [cargo capacity], from the West Indies, the northern states, Pensacola, Mobile, Covington, Madisonville. . . ." The turning basin also provided a name for a street on its southern boundary that would one day become an icon for jazz fans: Basin Street. As was true in any number of other port cities, the area close

Sailing boats docked in the turning basin of the Carondelet Canal during the era of sail. Photographer unknown. Image courtesy of Charles L. Thompson Collection, Louisiana State University.

to this transportation hub proved to be profitable for prostitution—in the case of New Orleans, in the form of Storyville, which was located just to the west, and which would later be identified by historians as the birthplace of the great American art form, jazz.[3]

Even in those early days, however, some of the city's leaders were developing plans to connect the canal to the Mississippi River. In particular, the tract of land that would later become Canal Street was once intended to be an actual canal instead of a street. The land was reserved by the U.S. Congress, at the time of the Louisiana Purchase, as a place for the Orleans Navigation Company to dig a canal. The plan at that time, although it was never consummated, was for the new canal to connect the Mississippi River with the existing Carondelet Canal and Bayou St. John, providing a water route to Lake Pontchartrain. The proposed canal was never completed, for a relatively simple reason: water levels of the Mississippi River are not just variable but also considerably higher than those in Lake Pontchartrain and Bayou St. John, both of which are close to sea level, and canal-building technologies of the time had no way to cope with that fact. Still, the seed had been planted, and in subsequent decades, local politicians and engineers spent plenty of time contemplating the possibilities.

As drainage and transportation patterns in New Orleans changed—and as English-speaking or American settlers increasingly flowed into the city after the 1803 Louisiana Purchase—patterns of settlement and development also shifted. The new American businessmen proved to be an exception to the tendency for people in this region to be comfortable with diversity and cultural blending; the new Americans did not share the cultural values and heritage of the established French population, so assimilation became more problematic. Instead, English-speaking or American settlers gravitated "uptown," meaning upstream along the Mississippi, or across what is now Canal Street and to the west of the French Quarter. Like the French and other settlers who had come before them, however, the English-speaking settlers of the nineteenth century continued to lay out their communities along the relatively high ground provided by the natural levee of the river.[4]

The "uptown" elites may not have lived in the same section of the city as the previous French inhabitants, but they soon realized that the kinds of commercial advantages provided by the Carondelet Canal might also be helpful in their part of the city. By 1830, the newer elites were pushing to construct a second canal to serve the interests of their new urban district, and by the following year the New Orleans Canal and Banking Company was formed, with $4 million in capital. The company proposed to dig a "New Basin Canal," which would be about six miles long and much more difficult to build than the "Old Basin Canal." In another theme that would be played out in different ways in later years, the new canal was also planned to be larger than the older one, with a width of 60 feet—as compared to about 20 feet for the Carondelet Canal—and a depth of six feet.[5]

One of the major challenges involved the need for workers. Slaves may have been treated as though they had little value as human beings, but they were seen as having enough economic value that the backers of the canal looked instead for laborers whose lives were seen as literally "worth" less than those of the slaves. The people they recruited were the newly arriving Irish immigrants, most of them desperately poor, who were fleeing the British occupation of Ireland.

One way in which the human resources of the area interacted with the natural ones, unfortunately, had to do with disease. Yellow fever infested the swamps, and disease ravaged the workforce. This was not an era when economic elites were terribly worried about the health of workers in general, or about Irish workers in particular. As one indication of that fact, officials did not even bother to keep a count of their death toll. Subsequent estimates of deaths in the "digger" population, due to cholera, yellow fever, and other causes, range from 6,000 to 20,000. Some of those workers were literally buried as well as killed by the canal, being left in unmarked "graves" in the spoil banks created by the excavation. Still, despite the high death rates and low wages—and despite the fact that the canal was finished seven years before the time that is seen by many as the start of the truly terrible times for the Irish, when the potato blight hit Ireland in 1845—there were enough boatloads of desperate Irish workers willing to take the dollar-a-day jobs that, between 1832 and 1838, the entire New Basin Canal was excavated by Irish laborers, using technology that consisted of little more than hand tools and wheelbarrows. After the construction period ended, the surviving Irish immigrants made their own contributions to the rich ethnic mix of New Orleans, many of them moving into what at the time were the slums of the "Irish Channel" neighborhood along the river.[6]

When seen from today's perspective, the New Basin Canal was an absolute disaster, particularly in terms of worker safety and health. Still, at least from the perspective of that era—a time when literal human slavery was still solidly established in the region—the insensitivity of the economic elites to the lives of the laborers who built the basis for their prosperity may have been "just" an uncommonly stark example of a sadly common pattern. From the perspective of economic development, meanwhile, the new canal was a clear success. The New Basin Canal competed favorably for commerce with the smaller Carondelet Canal, and it became a major force in the development of the city. And as with the Carondelet Canal, local movers and shakers considered the idea of extending the New Basin Canal all the way to the Mississippi River, but the extension never took place, again for lack of technological capacity.[7]

The commercial importance of the two canals can be understood from Richard Campanella's calculations of the commodity movements on the canals in the year ending August 31, 1865. In a pattern that foreshadowed future developments, the larger New Basin Canal carried significantly more building materials such as lumber and bricks than did the older and smaller Carondelet Canal. With the possible exception of charcoal, it carried more commerce of most other types as well.[8]

Chugging Along

Over the next century, the city's actual patterns of growth would reflect not just the modifications of the local environment by growth-oriented leaders, but also the rich resources of the Mississippi River basin, combined with more than a little bit of fortuitous timing in the development of new technologies.

Of those two topics, the more straightforward one involves the phenomenal resources of the Mississippi River basin. The land area drained by the river and its tributaries is vast, including all or part of 31 of the 50 present-day states, or just over 40 percent of the total land area of the continental U.S. It stretches from parts of New York State through most of Montana, and it even takes in small fractions of two Canadian provinces. Equally important, it happens to include what may be the most productive farming region in the world.

In the years leading up to the Louisiana Purchase in 1803, American farmers had already begun to move west of the Appalachian Mountains, into the Ohio River valley and beyond. Once in the new territories, they began to take advantage of two facts. One is that the prairie soils of the Mississippi River basin are rich and well suited for farming. The other is the fact that water flows downhill. It was the second fact that made it relatively affordable to carry even heavy agricultural commodities down the Ohio and the Mississippi rivers to New Orleans.

Generally, the first transportation downstream was provided by "flatboats"—simple wooden barges that could be disassembled for lumber once they reached New Orleans. From there, traditional sailing vessels could carry on trade with other locations along the Gulf of Mexico and beyond. Transportation back upstream, however, was not quite so simple; in many cases, the flatboat captains would need to walk or ride a horse all the way back to the territories from which they came, sometimes a thousand or more miles away. Under the circumstances, it is easy to imagine the kind of interest that would have been generated by the vessel that came to characterize river transportation over the course of the nineteenth century—the steamboat.

From the perspective of New Orleans' new elites, the arrival of the steamboat was spectacularly well timed, coming less than a decade after the American acquisition of the Mississippi River Valley in 1803. The key breakthrough, however, came not with the invention and date that are still taught to schoolchildren—Robert Fulton's invention of the steamship *Clermont*, in 1807—since that ship made its voyages on New York's Hudson River. Instead, the boat that truly revolutionized American river transportation was the one that Fulton introduced four years later, in 1811. Although he built it in Pittsburgh, Pennsylvania, he tellingly named it the *New Orleans*—and he started the revolution by sending this vessel down the Ohio and the Mississippi rivers, all the way to the newly American city after which it had been named, attracting a good deal of publicity and attention along the way. The attention, and the success of Fulton's innovations, quickly led to the transformation of water transportation and commerce for the entire stretch of the still-new nation that lay to the west of the Appalachian Mountains.[9]

In his classic 1949 study of the great age of steamboats, Louis C. Hunter notes that

> The western steamboat . . . through a process of elimination, adaptation, and accretion, gradually lost all but the most generalized resemblance to a ship and became a fresh-water, shallow-river vessel. . . . The keel disappeared, the hull lost depth, and the superstructure mounted higher and higher.[10]

Steamboats came in all sizes and shapes, ranging from as small as 20 tons to over 500 tons, but they were characteristically driven by paddle wheels, for several reasons. First, rivers were often filled with snags and debris. Given that paddle wheels extended only a short distance into the water, they were less likely to be damaged by snags than a more traditional "screw" or propeller. If damaged, the wheel was easy to repair, because the paddles were made of wood that could easily be replaced through locally available supplies, and the damaged part could be rotated above the water for easy access. Second, the Mississippi and its tributaries are often shallow and filled with sandbars, and paddles required less draft than the large screws used on oceangoing vessels. Finally, unlike screws, paddle wheels operated equally well in reverse—an important consideration for vessels that made frequent bow-on or nose-in landings along the river.

Most of the early steamboats were side-wheelers, as this design allowed the heavy machinery to be concentrated in the center of the boat, where the hull was strongest. It also allowed greater maneuverability, since the paddle wheels could be made to turn in opposite directions, giving the boat a turning radius equal to its length. As improvements in design led to structurally stronger hulls, however, increasing numbers of larger and larger stern-wheelers appeared, with the stern-wheelers eventually becoming the workhorses of the Mississippi River.

At a minimum, the "inevitable" emergence of New Orleans needs to be understood in terms of the historically specific interactions that took place between the city's natural setting and the technologies that were becoming available to take advantage of it. The location of New Orleans did provide important strategic advantages, but it was thanks to the steamboats as well as to its own location that New Orleans would ultimately come to dominate the trade along the entire Mississippi River Valley. To give local leaders their due, however, it was also their hard work that would help to make New Orleans and the associated port facilities, extending along the adjacent riverbanks in both directions, the nation's busiest port complex—a distinction that the port facilities of southern Louisiana continue to enjoy today.[11]

⌐ Chapter 4 *⌐*

The Growth Machine
Comes to New Orleans

O NE OF THE NAMES that will be familiar to anyone who has
spent time in New Orleans belongs to a hero of the War of
1812 who was also one of the city's most famous celebrities
during its early years—Jean Lafitte. Lafitte, an early entrepreneur,
was a pirate—or as he preferred it, a "privateer." As such, his career
involved an ambiguous relationship between virtue and villainy—and
an equally ambiguous relationship with economic development.

For years, Lafitte and his crew carried out their business activities
from his base on Grand Terre, a barrier island on the Gulf of Mexico
about 40 miles south of New Orleans. He obtained most of his wares
from Spanish ships that he plundered in the Caribbean and Atlantic;
he and his crews then sold the "goods" they obtained, including slaves,
luxury items, and more, to customers who lived in New Orleans and
the surrounding region.[1]

In a way that seems somehow appropriate for this region, Lafitte
was a complicated as well as legendary character. Although his base
on Grand Terre was attacked and destroyed by a small fleet of gun-
boats from the U.S. Navy, led by the short-lived US Schooner *Carolina*, in September of 1814, Lafitte showed up soon thereafter to assist
U.S. forces, led by Andrew Jackson, in resisting an invasion by British

forces. Lafitte's help was a significant factor in the American victory in the Battle of New Orleans, which actually took place on the plains of Chalmette, at a bottleneck between the river and the Rodriguez Canal, several miles downstream from the Vieux Carre, in January of 1815. Following the battle, Lafitte moved his base of operations to the "Neutral Strip"—a forty-mile-wide stretch of wilderness and marshland between the Sabine and the Calcasieu rivers, which was left in a kind of limbo as the result of a boundary dispute relating to the 1806 treaty between Spanish Texas and the United States. Given that the agreement left the Strip unoccupied by troops and law enforcement officials of either nation, Lafitte was happy to fill the vacuum, although he turned the focus of his commercial endeavors toward Galveston in later years.

Lafitte was a pirate and a slave trader, but even in his own time he was often seen as a romantic figure, at least by the white local citizens. Today, nearly two hundred years later, tourists who come to the French Quarter of New Orleans can find the visitor center and headquarters for the National Park Service sites that are named after him—the Jean Lafitte National Historical Park and Preserve. His example is worth keeping in mind, not just as a historical footnote, but as a way of providing context for considering the local leaders who have done the most to shape the city and its surroundings in the years since he headed west to Galveston.

In some ways, Lafitte would seem to have less in common with the later leaders of New Orleans than with the more colorful leaders who emerged elsewhere in America a century later—the "robber barons," such as Cornelius Vanderbilt and John D. Rockefeller, who built vast fortunes with shipping and oil. Like Lafitte, these larger-than-life men were enormously wealthy, remembered more for power over major industries than for careful compliance with all the relevant laws. The local leaders in New Orleans who came after Lafitte, by contrast, were less romantic and more legal.

Still, in many ways, Lafitte's real heirs were indeed the later leaders of New Orleans.

One way of thinking about Lafitte's commercial activities is that he contributed at least modestly to the economic development of New Orleans by bringing in outside "subsidies"—plundered goods of all sorts that in some cases were available only to New Orleanians through his activities and that in other cases could be sold for lower prices than would have been available otherwise. In many ways, what we have come to expect from our local leaders in more recent times is that they, too, bring in "subsidies," but of a different sort. Lafitte's subsidies were made possible through old-fashioned thievery, while more recent leaders have been more likely to pursue the kinds of subsidies called "economic development" investments by their proponents—or called "pork barrel" projects by their opponents. Many such undertakings—projects such as levees and canals, or for that matter, bridges and interstate highway interchanges—are seen in part as ways to bring federal dollars to one state or congressional district from taxpayers all across the nation. Such present-day activities by local leaders are thus not just legal, but are in some ways blessed by the legal system, being made possible by friendly lawmakers at higher levels of government.

While not every city has had its Lafitte, most American cities today do have leaders who are trying to pull in the pork. Decades ago, the more modern way of bringing in "subsidies" had become so widespread that professor Harvey Molotch argued that a typical American city could be understood as the "expression of the interests of some land-based elite ... compet[ing] ... to have growth-inducing resources invested within its own area." In Molotch's analysis—and certainly in the eyes of local leaders—there is almost nothing "inevitable" about the ways in which a city will grow and develop. Instead, today's development-oriented or "land-based" elites focus heavily on bringing in the kinds of external resources that they believe will enhance their cities' economic prospects, in at least a rough analogue to the ways in which external resources of plunder and slaves were brought in by Lafitte's earlier "sea-based" privateers. The net result, Molotch has argued, is that "the political and economic essence of virtually any given locality, in the present American context, is growth." In light of that observation, Molotch also gave this perspective its name, noting that the process tended to turn a typical American city into a "Growth Machine."[2]

An important catch, though, is that all of these efforts to promote "growth" may actually result in something else.

The common expectation is that urban citizens are so interested in economic development that they will be willing to accept whatever costs will result from the promotion of growth—including any environmental costs. Even in academic literature, there has long been an inclination to view environmental harm as an inevitable by-product of economic expansion. As will become clear on closer consideration of the human tragedy of Katrina, however, it may be particularly important to take a closer look at the assumption that the activities creating environmental harm are likely to lead to increased economic vitality.[3]

Lafitte offers a straightforward illustration of the reasons why greater scrutiny is needed. A reasonably safe assumption is that the citizens who bought his plundered goods or slaves thought of him as offering a useful economic service, while those who originally shipped the same goods or slaves—the persons from whom the cargoes were plundered—would have disagreed quite strongly. Attitudes toward modern-day Somali pirates are in some ways similar: it stands to reason that the piracy-related incomes would be welcome in a poor nation such as Somalia, but elsewhere, world leaders have been uncommonly united in denouncing the piracy as an intolerable threat to trade and the world economy.

Almost any neutral economic analysis, meanwhile, would be likely to agree with the world leaders in this case, judging the net or overall effects of piracy and plunder to be bad, not good, for the overall economy. In slightly more technical language, the "subsidies" brought in by privateers, as well as those brought in more recently by Growth Machine leaders, will generally "lessen economic efficiency," in economists' terminology, doing more harm than good for the economy as a whole. A few people make out like bandits—in Lafitte's case, literally so. A number of others might seem to benefit more modestly—for example, from the fact that stolen goods will normally sell at lower prices than will the products associated with legal commerce. In overall terms, however, economists tell us that the net costs of thievery, and of other kinds of "subsidies" and distortions in free-market systems, tend to be significantly greater than the benefits.

In recent years, accordingly, a growing number of researchers have started to question the common assumption that local promotion of "growth" will indeed contribute to the economy. Smaller but growing numbers of those researchers have become increasingly skeptical toward the idea that environmental harm, more broadly, is an unavoidable by-product of economic expansion. Their skepticism, moreover, appears to be warranted. To the extent to which the relationship has been examined, rather than simply assumed, the evidence fails to support the common assumption that environmentally damaging projects "must" be good for the economy. Instead, it turns out that much or most of the environmental harm in the U.S. is highly disproportionate to actual levels of economic activity.

Despite the tendency of many politicians to back environmentally damaging projects because of their presumed importance for "jobs," the most damaging projects tend to be especially unimpressive with respect to actual employment numbers. The majority of toxic emissions in the United States, for example, come not from the most vital sectors of U.S. industry, but from industries that make up only about 4 percent of the economy—and as if to make things worse, they support barely 1 percent of the jobs. Rather than representing a conflict between "the economy" and the environment, the actual patterns of environmental harm might better be understood as representing a conflict between what "everyone knows" and *what the evidence shows.*[4]

The nature of the relationship between economic vitality and environmental harm has long been particularly important in New Orleans. Local elites in the Crescent City have focused on water projects and canals in their efforts to promote "economic development," but as will be spelled out in the next several chapters, those efforts have done as little to promote genuine economic development, especially in recent decades, as did the earlier plundering by Lafitte and his men. A more careful look at the actual outcomes of their activities, moreover, can teach us a good deal about why the city's citizens would have suffered so painfully from the power of Katrina.

A useful starting point for that analysis is to take a closer look at the early city map that was shown in chapter 2. In 1798, the entire city covered just a few city blocks—the area that we know today as the French Quarter. For the mapmaker's purposes, it was important to show not just those city blocks but also the bodies of water in the vicinity, including not just the Mississippi River but also Bayou St. John, as well as early drainage canals. Notably, although the streets of the then-new city were laid out on the kind of grid that would seem familiar today in the Midwestern farm towns to the north, higher up the Mississippi River Valley, the founders of New Orleans saw no reason to align their streets with the compass. Instead, the streets of early New Orleans lined up with the river. On that early map, accordingly, "north" is roughly 45 degrees off-kilter—the top of the map is oriented toward the northwest. Even today, directions in New Orleans are usually stated not in terms of compass coordinates, but in terms of heading toward or away from the river—and "up" means "upstream," not north. Something else about that early map, on the other hand, reveals a particularly dramatic change. Two hundred years ago, the city's crescent of land along the Mississippi, bounded on one side by the river itself, was bounded on all other sides by healthy cypress swamps. At the time, they provided not just lumber but also protection from storms. Today, they no longer do. Therein lies a story.

Carving the Marshes

Within a few years of the first European settlement in the area, as noted above, local leaders sought to improve their economic prospects by building canals. Particularly during the city's early years, when local citizens were investing their own money instead of trying to attract pork-barrel funding from distant politicians, those efforts do indeed seem to have contributed to the city's prosperity. During the years when the Carondelet and the New Basin canals were in use, however, emerging national trends in waterborne commerce were undermining as well as reinforcing the canals' importance.

In terms of the technology that was available when they were constructed, the two canals were respectable achievements. Even as late as 1816, there were just 100 miles of canals in the United States—the longest being the Middlesex Canal, linking Boston Harbor with the farmlands to the north of that city. The staples of an expanding farm economy were bulk agricultural commodities, which had a high ratio of weight to value, and the only way to carry them over long distances, cheaply, was by water. That fact eventually led a growing number of people to have more or less the same idea. In the words of *The Encyclopedia of American History*,

> In the period from the mid-1820s to the Civil War . . . the United States underwent a vast expansion of canal construction, becoming the world's leading nation in both mileage of canals and the volume of tonnage carried on them. The canal lines were of crucial importance in the integration of a national economy, and they played a key role in the so-called Transportation Revolution that expedited both westward expansion and a robust industrialization process in the North and West.[5]

The "transportation revolution" associated with canal-building initially brought prosperity to the city near the mouth of the nation's most important river system, but within a few decades, the patterns began to change. The "revolution" shifted first to railroads and then to the highways that could accommodate the internal combustion engine—developments that would carry different implications altogether. New Orleans was the third-largest city in the U.S. in 1840, but by the end of the century, with railroads replacing the rivers as the major transportation routes, it had dropped to twelfth place. By the later years of the nineteenth century, the community leaders of New Orleans were thus growing increasingly concerned about prospects for maintaining the city's transportation prominence.[6]

The Carondelet and the New Basin canals continued to carry some commerce into the twentieth century, but gradually—as goods came increasingly to be transported by rail, trucks, and larger vessels—both of the early canals were becoming obsolete. Under the circumstances, local leaders also had good reason not to trust the future prosperity of New Orleans to what geographers call the city's natural "situation." Instead, they agreed with a speech that would be given a few years later by Jared Sanders—one of many Louisiana governors who was a great friend of "the triumphant march of progress" in New Orleans—speaking, ironically enough, at a feast to celebrate the building of a railroad, although the railroad had been built to serve the city's port facilities. "While there are these great natural outlets," he observed, "commerce seeks the channel of the least resistance." What that meant, he said, was that if New Orleans wished to enjoy the "great advantages" provided to the city by nature, then "man must come to its assistance."[7]

When they came up with plans for that assistance, they did so with a vengeance.

Like local leaders of earlier times, those of the late nineteenth century dreamed in particular of "coming to the assistance" of nature by digging a direct water connection from the Mississippi River down to Lake Pontchartrain. The dream would have to wait until most commercial uses of steamboats had come to an end—save perhaps for transporting tourists—but it was one that would not die. The key problems that delayed the dream had to do not with the will, but with the way.

As noted above, the problem that had stymied earlier canals was that water levels of the Mississippi River were much higher and much more variable than those of Lake Pontchartrain. That difference, in turn, can be traced to the processes by which rivers build land in a generally flat region such as southern Louisiana, often leaving a narrow strip of (relatively) high ground quite close to the river itself—including the "sliver by the river" that was the obvious place for building a city such as New Orleans. Over time, thanks to the buildup of natural levees through periodic flooding, both the levees and the river can actually come to be perched above the surrounding countryside. This is the case with the Mississippi River at New Orleans, where patterns of rainfall and upstream snowmelt mean that the river's surface level can often fluctuate over a fifteen-foot range. Even the lower end of that range, however, is well above the surface level of Lake Pontchartrain, which as noted above, is close to the level of the Gulf of Mexico—that is, sea level.

A lock system that could accommodate such a degree of fluctuation was not technologically possible during the eighteenth and nineteenth centuries. By the dawn of the twentieth century, however, the available know-how was finally up to the task, and it was put to work in the excavation of a new canal—this one connecting to another brackish "lake" that lies to the east rather than the north of New Orleans—Lake Borgne.

Sensibly enough, this new waterway was known as the Lake Borgne Canal, although it was later called the Violet Canal, in honor of the small nearby community of Violet. The new canal, which was also undertaken as a private venture, made use of another bayou that originally drained the "back side" of the levee along the Mississippi River, just below New Orleans, heading toward the east—Bayou Dupré. The bayou was widened and a lock was constructed, allowing vessels to go from the Mississippi River to Lake Borgne. From there, vessels could connect either to the Gulf of Mexico, to the southeast, or into Lake Pontchartrain, to the north.

With the completion of the Lake Borgne Canal in 1904, just over a century after the Louisiana Purchase, the long-dreamed water connection was finally a reality. The new canal attracted attention from as far away as the *New York Times*, which predicted on November 24, 1900, that "the Lake Borgne Canal, which will connect the Mississippi Sound and the rivers of Alabama with the Mississippi River at New Orleans, will be completed shortly." The *Times* was especially impressed with the possibility that the new canal would lead to large reductions in the prices for southern yellow pine in St. Louis and even Chicago.[8]

In a pattern that perhaps should have received more attention than it did, however, this historic, long-sought achievement was soon merely a historical footnote. Although there was some traffic on this route in the early twentieth century, the 40-foot-wide lock that connected the canal to the Mississippi River soon proved to be too small to accommodate growing vessel sizes. Within a few years of the time when the long-sought canal was finally opened, traffic tapered off, and the Lake Borgne Canal was soon abandoned as obsolete.

Obsolete on Delivery?

This story illustrates a pattern that deserves closer attention. The Carondelet Canal was opened before 1800, and the New Basin Canal by the 1830s. Both canals were in operation for over a century, continuing to see use even after the construction of the Lake Borgne Canal. The newer canal, by contrast, had a much shorter useful life.

This difference implies that it would be useful to examine the length of the period between the opening of a project and the time when it becomes obsolete, or what could be called its working life.

The issue is one that takes on special importance during times when technology is undergoing rapid change. Particularly if we are considering large projects that take considerable time to build, we may need to consider the possibility that the working life of a project, or the time between its implementation and obsolescence, could ultimately shrink to the vanishing point. As we will soon spell out, perhaps the most ironic and most regrettable example would be one involving a long-sought and environmentally damaging project—one that takes an especially long time to build, precisely because it is so large and expensive—that has effectively become obsolete by the time it is completed or delivered.

The "obsolete on delivery" phenomenon can arise in any number of contexts, but it stands to reason that such a pattern might be particularly pronounced in the case of projects that involve a single-minded, long-term focus on something that Molotch saw as one of the key components of Growth Machine dynamics—the ongoing effort to attract funding from higher levels of government.

The reason is easy to describe but not so easy to counteract. Given that all of us have difficulty imagining a future that has not yet arrived, most projects are designed to meet current conditions, or what we can foresee as "likely" future conditions—that is, those that are sufficiently similar to current conditions that they seem plausible to project designers. The challenges of looking into the future may be especially great when a project is pushing the limits of available technology, meaning not only that project planners will have no real experience to draw upon in evaluating possibilities, but also that even moderately similar experiences may be limited or nonexistent.

One unfortunate implication is that unless technological development is utterly stagnant, then by the time major projects can be conceived, politically supported, funded, and built, the technologies they were intended to serve may no longer exist. The more massive the project, the longer it takes to be completed, and the more fast-changing the technology, the greater is the likelihood that the project will have become obsolete by the time it is delivered or completed.

Water transport is rarely seen as a hotbed of modern technological innovation, but it has not been entirely stagnant, and for that reason, the canals of New Orleans offer a clear illustration of how projects can become "obsolete on delivery."

In some senses, the guiding principle of water transportation today—namely that even the heaviest cargo can float if the ship is large enough—is one that would have made sense well before the era of Mark Twain and *Huckleberry Finn*. The advantages of water transport are greatest when cargoes are heaviest: the buoyancy of a sufficiently large vessel allows even the heaviest of cargoes to be transported relatively cheaply by water. In another sense, however, one of the long-established patterns of change in water transportation— the trend toward ever-larger ships—is one that took on considerably increased importance over the course of the twentieth century.

Wood floats far better than metal, so the idea of building ships from steel is one that took some time to catch on. Once shipbuilders began to master the art of constructing their ships from iron and steel, however—something that took place largely in the twentieth century—ships could take on entirely new dimensions. The expansion of ships' sizes and capacities became particularly pronounced after the end of World War II, led by developments in Japan, where recovery from the wartime devastation relied in part on the construction of entirely new facilities, both for iron and steel production and also for shipbuilding.[9]

The growth promoters of New Orleans were intent on building new canals, but during a time of change, a canal that would have been more than large enough to serve the dominant ships of one generation could quickly become too small to be of much use to the ships of the next. Unfortunately, rather than keeping a careful eye on these unfolding trends in shipbuilding—which may well have seemed to be a world away at the time—local growth promoters mainly kept their focus on promoting the same ideas that their predecessors had been promoting decades earlier.

The implications of that problem are illustrated by two more canals. One of them—the project officially known as the "Inner Harbor Navigation Canal," but more commonly known by locals simply as the "Industrial Canal"—went through a decade-long period of planning and construction during the early twentieth century, and it narrowly escaped the fate of being obsolete on delivery. Unfortunately, the project that it spawned—the Mississippi River–Gulf Outlet or MRGO, with a planning/construction window that spanned some four decades, during the middle of the century—did not. What that later project would do instead would be to play a major role in the tragedy that later generations would come to know as Katrina.

⁓ Chapter 5 ⁓

A "Helpful Explosion"

*F*ORMALLY LEGISLATED efforts by "men" to "come to the
assistance of nature" in New Orleans are nearly as old as
the city, but they took on a new level of intensity at the end
of the nineteenth century. In 1895, "the New Orleans Board of
Trade, considered the most powerful business association in the city
from 1879 to 1928, organized a conference to 'investigate' the conditions of the port," and a lawyer and former head of the city's cotton
exchange, Walter Flowers, was elected as the city's mayor. The new
mayor wasted no time in demonstrating his commitment to the city's
commercial interests, and he soon managed to line up important
allies in the state capital, particularly when the issue was waterfront
reform.[1]

By the very next year, 1896, the recommendations from the Board
of Trade Conference had been blessed by the state legislature, becoming what is officially recorded as Louisiana Act 70. Among its other
features, the legislation established the Board of Commissioners for
the Port of New Orleans, locally known as the "Dock Board," to
administer the city's wharves, build new ones, and to "erect sheds
thereon to protect merchandise in transit."[2]

The legislation not only specified that all commissioners must
be "predominantly identified with the commerce or business interest of the port of New Orleans," but it also made the Dock Board
dependent on the fees that could be obtained from property and from

facilities that used the public waterways. From the start, in short, the Dock Board was a creature of the Growth Machine. A few years later, inspired by the opening of the Panama Canal, the Louisiana legislature further reinforced the identification with business interests by adding provisions for the Dock Board to expropriate property and issue bonds for a larger canal in New Orleans.[3]

Thomas Dabney, who was employed by the Dock Board to write an account of the building of the Industrial Canal, described the canal's location in a passage that made no mention of political considerations, but instead seemed to make the Industrial Canal almost as "natural" or inevitable a part of the landscape as the cypress trees:

> There is a map in the possession of T. P. Thompson of New Orleans, who has a notable collection of books and documents on the early history of this city, dated March 1, 1827, and drawn by Captain W. T. Possin, topographical engineer, showing the route of a proposed canal to connect the Mississippi River and Lake Pontchartrain, curiously near the site finally chosen for the great enterprise nearly a hundred years later.[4]

On the ground, meanwhile, a powerful city-wide coalition of elite interests had been pursuing the idea of a new canal in a much more down-to-earth way. The City Shipbuilding Committee, which began meeting early in 1918, included just one elected official—the mayor— along with assorted bankers and financiers, representatives of three local newspapers, and the superintendent of the Sewerage and Water Board. This was one committee that appears to have spent little time in debate. Dabney reported that, by February 10, 1918, about a month after being formed, the committee had "laid the plans for an industrial basin, connected with the river by a lock, and ultimately to be connected with the lake by a small barge canal," which would be known later as the Industrial Canal.[5]

In the early days of the twentieth century, New Orleans was still a major port, but it was also still focused on the Mississippi River, and by this time, local growth promoters had their eyes on bigger things. The reasons why Dabney would have called attention to a "Shipbuilding Committee" involves an additional consideration: as shipbuilding was moving toward ever-larger steel construction, those ships were becoming increasingly difficult to build on the Mississippi

River. Large-scale shipbuilding required huge "marine ways"—sloped marine railways—to hold the vessels during construction and then launch them into the water when the hulls were basically complete. Because river levels fluctuated widely across seasons and in response to changes in precipitation upstream, the marine ways would have to be long enough that the shipbuilding could be done well above the surface of the river, even at high water, while still reaching low enough that it would be possible to launch the ships even during low water. Those marine ways would also have to be constructed so as to avoid conflicts with shipping traffic—and finally, they would also have to be stout enough to avoid the problem of being carved away by the river, even during times of the highest and fastest river flows.

By contrast, the alternative that local interests envisioned was one that seemed to offer hope for renewed shipbuilding in the New Orleans area. The Industrial Canal would basically stay at sea level—but that was only one of its attractions. Another consideration was that, under Louisiana law, the banks of rivers and other "major water-ways" were public land, while the banks of canals were not. Part of the appeal of the Industrial Canal was thus that it would allow the properties on the new canal to be privately owned, and taxed. Powerful interests in the maritime sector—including not just shipbuilders but salvage companies, towing companies, and various types of warehousing enterprises—were eager to acquire space that could offer them the best of both worlds, being private land while still being connected directly to the Mississippi. The Dock Board was equally eager to start collecting fees from them.

Well before Dabney wrote his account, the Louisiana legislature had already demonstrated its support for increased commerce in New Orleans, having passed an act on July 9, 1914, that authorized the Board of Commissioners of Louisiana to build a small barge and industrial canal. At just about that time, however—despite the intensity of local and even state-wide interest—World War I had interrupted the process. Still, the interruption may have been fortunate. The original plan for the Industrial Canal was for the lock to accommodate vessels with a "draft," or a distance between the water line and the bottom of the ship, of 16–18 feet. Once construction actually started, however, the lock project was approximately doubled in size and depth, responding to the fact that ships were growing in size. Had construction not been halted by World War I, the Industrial Canal might well have been built to its originally planned dimensions, meaning that it might have become obsolete just as quickly as did the Lake Borgne Canal before it.[6]

Thanks to the expansion of the original plans, however, the Industrial Canal was a state-of-the-art accomplishment by the time it was finally finished in 1923. It featured one of the largest locks in the country—640 feet long by 74 feet wide by 31.5 feet deep—accommodating even the larger vessels of that time. Unfortunately, even the last-minute expansion would ultimately increase the project's useful lifetime only modestly.

The territory to be crossed by the Industrial Canal was not exactly a center of urban development at the time; instead, it was home to a fairly dense stand of cypress trees. In the initial decades after its construction, however, the "Inner Harbor" of the Industrial Canal—a harbor that was inside the city and a short distance away from the banks of the Mississippi—would indeed become the kind of busy place envisioned by Growth Machine proponents. By the time the Army Corps of Engineers had produced the map of the canal that is even today shown on its website (despite depicting a level of economic activity dramatically greater than what has actually existed for many years), the canal would be lined by more than fifty businesses.[7]

Part of the reason for its initial success is that, soon after its completion, the Industrial Canal also became a part of the growing Gulf Intracoastal Waterway (GIWW) system, which gets its name from the fact that it allowed ships to move goods "inside" the coast of the Gulf of Mexico, sheltered from open-water conditions by barrier islands and by the excavation of still more canals. The GIWW offered a mostly inland pathway across the Florida panhandle to the mouth of Mobile Bay. From there, it traced the same route that had been used by the early French explorers, behind the barrier islands off Alabama and Mississippi and into Lake Pontchartrain, where a nine-foot-deep channel was dredged to the entrance of the Industrial Canal, allowing shipments to reach the Mississippi River through the new lock.

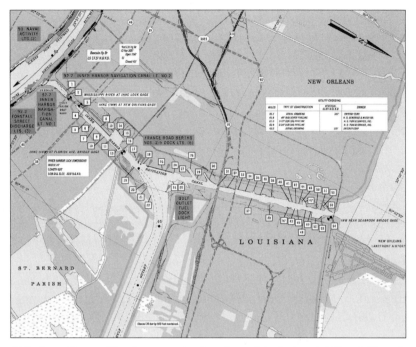

U.S. Army Corps of Engineers navigation chart of the Industrial Canal. Note the numbered boxes, indicating the many businesses that once lined the canal. On this map, north is to the right.

The portion of the GIWW that crossed the lake, unfortunately, was problematic from the beginning. It was narrow, and obviously it was limited to vessels of less than a nine-foot draft. In addition, channels across shallow bays and estuaries are notoriously difficult to maintain, because wave and current action contribute to rapid siltation. The correction of this problematic portion of the GIWW would play a role in the eventual excavation of an even larger navigation project.

Even before the completion of the Industrial Canal in the early 1920s, local boosters went to work on a new undertaking, trying to induce the federal government to take over the operation and maintenance of the Industrial Canal, primarily so the lock could be operated toll-free, encouraging traffic movement along the coast. These efforts intensified during World War II, thanks in large part to the influence of the most important of the shipbuilding enterprises along the Industrial Canal—a mile-long plant owned by A. J. Higgins, who happened to be a member of the Dock Board as well as the Levee Board. The vessels built there, known as "Higgins Boats"—the official name was "Landing Craft, Vehicle, Personnel (LCVP)"—made good use of lessons that could be learned from navigating through the shallow waters of Louisiana wetlands. The result was the landing craft that played an important role in the D-Day invasion of Normandy, as well as in other amphibious landings around the globe, from North Africa to the South Pacific.

Although Higgins insisted that the plant would also continue to prosper after the war, it was as part of the war effort that the Higgins company built a new "Liberty Plant" about a mile away from the Industrial Canal facility, at a location locals know as Michaud, and then dredged a new canal to connect the two plants, beginning in 1942. In response to congressional authorization that came that same year, the Army Corps of Engineers began enlarging the GIWW. In short order, the GIWW was officially routed through the new Higgins waterway and into the Industrial Canal—and soon thereafter came efforts to build something much larger.[8]

In some respects, those efforts were already well under way by that time. In the same year as Dabney's 1921 publication, for example, a less-widely noticed pamphlet summarized "Policies of the Board of Commissioners of the Port of New Orleans for The Inner Harbor Navigation Canal." Included in that pamphlet was not just a map of the still-incomplete canal but also a "Proposed Deep Sea Canal" leaving the Industrial Canal to the east. In the words of the pamphlet, "the Board became convinced that the Industrial Canal should be considered as the first step toward a canal to the sea" and that the "Federal Government should be urged to undertake the work of creating such a canal at the earliest possible date."[9]

By the 1940s, the *Eureka News Bulletin*—the official newsletter for Higgins employees—was particularly clear in its prediction that the canal being dredged to the Higgins plant in Michaud would eventually "be continued from the Higgins plant to the Gulf of Mexico. When this is completed, New Orleans' dream for more than a century will be realized." As spelled out in previous chapters, the leaders

Artist's conception of the Industrial Canal, as depicted in the "Policies of the Board of Commissioners of the Port of New Orleans for The Inner Harbor Navigation Canal," published in 1921. Note the "Proposed Deep Sea Canal," to the east of the Canal, roughly where the Mississippi River–Gulf Outlet and Gulf Intracoastal Waterway would later be constructed.

of New Orleans had in fact long dreamed of a canal that would make New Orleans a seaport, rather than simply a "river town," more than 100 miles from the Gulf. Still, it was the completion of the Industrial Canal, combined with new political opportunities, that seemed to offer for the first time a realistic possibility of achieving that dream. This time, local leaders wanted to build a long-discussed shortcut not just to the relatively shallow waters of Lake Pontchatrain, but all the way to the Gulf of Mexico.[10]

Reflecting their aspirations to become a "real" seaport city, they now referred to the proposal as a "tidewater" canal. One of the organizations they set up to lead the charge, similarly, was called the Tidewater Development Association. One of its leading members was Col. Lester F. Alexander, who had previously worked as an engineer for the U.S. Army Corps of Engineers, focusing on the lower Mississippi River. After leaving the federal government, Colonel Alexander started his own contracting firm as well as a shipbuilding company on the Industrial Canal. In the words of one analyst, "His role demonstrates not only the institutional linkage between the private sector, the Port of New Orleans, and the federal government; his investment on the Industrial Canal gave Alexander a direct financial interest in a project that would increase the value of his property." Another notable member of the Tidewater Development Association was A. B. Freeman, who came from "the highest echelons of the New Orleans social aristocracy. . . . He worked as a Coca-Cola executive and founded Wesson Oil. He also served as a port commissioner, held membership in the most exclusive social club in the city (Boston Club), and served on the Tulane Board of Trustees."[11]

Coordinating its activities with the Dock Board, the Association went to work with considerable energy to get state and especially federal agencies to share the local dream of a new sea-level shortcut to the Gulf. Part of their enthusiasm for a new waterway, presumably, stemmed from the fact that many of the local leaders would have been old enough to remember the times during the nineteenth century when siltation and snags had created real shipping challenges downriver from the city. Perhaps another part of the reason, however, may have been the fact that, rather than thinking about building this canal by using local financing, as had been the pattern in the past, they saw the new canal as a way of spending someone else's money.

Bigger and Better?

Strictly speaking, the idea of obtaining federal funding for water projects such as dams and canals was not a new concept at the time. During the early years of the nineteenth century, the national government had used such projects as a way to buy the loyalties of local elites in faraway regions. By paying for water projects that were too large to be financed locally, the federal government could help to assure that even the more remote territories would see good reasons for remaining part of the union. The idea gained extra currency after gold was discovered in California in 1848, a full continent away from the national capital, and especially after the 1860s, when the Civil War demonstrated the terrible costs of using military force to prevent secession from the "United" States. With the coming of the New Deal years in the 1930s, however, the amount of funding available for water-related construction projects would rise to an entirely new level.[12]

Part of the official logic behind such capital-intensive projects has always been that, although their expenses might go beyond the financial capacities of remote and less-developed territories, they would contribute to national as well as local prosperity. Part of the unofficial logic may have been that—even in cases where the projects would have brought their benefits almost exclusively to a smaller number of local elites, rather than to local or regional economies more broadly—the projects could usually expect to generate little opposition, especially in the poorer and more rural areas where most of them were built.* It may well be at least as true for the flow of government funds as for the flow of Mississippi River waters, though, that once a stream has been started and a channel has been carved, the early trickles tend to be followed by greater and greater flows over the years that follow, meaning that the channels often grow but can be very difficult to shut off.

By contrast, the moving of heaven, or at least of earth, seems to have been considerably more straightforward.

Much of the earth-moving was done by an agency that came under considerable scrutiny after Katrina, namely the U.S. Army Corps of Engineers—an agency recorded as USACE in the agency's own bureaucratic accounts, but generally called "the Corps" in everyday conversations. The origins of the Corps can be traced back to the time when specialists were hired to build military projects during the Revolutionary War, but in the nineteenth century, the agency's

---

*In more technical literature, two of the authors of this volume have discussed some of the key reasons why this phenomenon may be more pronounced in rural areas. First, rural areas tend to have high levels of what social science journals call "densities of acquaintanceship," meaning relatively high fractions of local people who know one another. Second, and in part because of the first reason, even projects that generate benefits only for a subset of the people in such a region tend to have high "social multiplier effects." That is, even the people who do not derive a direct benefit themselves will tend to be highly unlikely to oppose projects that are bringing prosperity to their friends and neighbors. For further discussion, see Freudenburg (1986); also Freudenburg and Gramling (1994).

responsibilities grew to include extensive involvement in civilian transportation projects. A later and further expansion of its responsibilities took place more abruptly: after the extensive flooding of 1927, which brought disastrous flooding along much of the length of the Mississippi River, the building of levees for flood control became a major responsibility of the Corps.[13]

Despite the criticism it would later attract, the Corps of Engineers does appear to have tried hard during its earlier years to make rational decisions about such investments. In fact, the Corps began using formal cost-benefit analysis as part of an efficiency movement during the Progressive Era—a period that, to the initial inconvenience of the New Orleans Dock Board, lasted from the 1890s through the 1920s.

A useful starting point for considering cost-benefit analysis—or what the Corps generally calls benefit-cost analysis—is the Rivers and Harbors Act. According to that legislation, which Congress passed in 1902, at a time when the Corps of Engineers was still highly respected for its professionalism, the agency needed to certify water projects as being sufficiently beneficial to be worth undertaking. At least at first, the process seems to have been a rigorous one, with more than half of the proposed projects being rejected, generally on grounds of unfavorable economic characteristics. By the 1920s, an amendment to the act seemed to tighten the reforms, explicitly requiring that the benefits be greater than the costs. Further reforms were enacted during the New Deal era, including the Federal Navigation Act of 1936, which mandated new safeguards to ensure that water-project investments would bring the maximum feasible economic benefit to a nation that needed badly to recover from the Great Depression. Perhaps tellingly, however, the 1936 Act was in turn a response to the fact that—despite the safeguards already in place by then—water-development projects had already become notorious for pork-barrel scrambles.[14]

The new requirements also had some effect on the Dock Board's quest for congressional funding. The key decision-making body—formally known as the Board of Engineers of the U.S. Army Corps of Engineers—responded to initial requests for the federal takeover of the Industrial Canal by ruling that there was not enough traffic to justify the request. In a decision that was in some ways prescient, the

Board of Engineers took special note of the fact that "incorporation of the Industrial Canal into the federal intracoastal waterway project [had] become caught up in another issue involving *construction of an alternative deep-water outlet from the Mississippi River to the Gulf,* also not considered necessary [by the Corps] at that time." This "alternative deep-water outlet" was the "Tidewater Canal" project envisioned by local proponents, which later generations would come to know as the "Mississippi River–Gulf Outlet," or MRGO. At least in 1936, however, the agency's blunt assessment was that there was "no necessity for another deep-water outlet from the Mississippi River." [15]

If this lack of enthusiasm from the Chief of Engineers did actually bother the local boosters, they seemed not to show it. Instead, the Dock Board and its allies went to work. Their first task was to convince the Corps that the project enjoyed fervent local support—a task in which local newspapers seemed only too ready to participate. With a degree of intensity notable even in the context of other growth-promotion efforts of this era, the *New Orleans Item,* for example, editorialized that "the port's lifeline should not depend entirely upon a crooked, fog-covered, silt-bearing, temperamental river channel, which might otherwise restrain or restrict the growth of the port of New Orleans like a Chinese girl's foot." [16]

The next task was to convince the Corps that this project would bring economic benefits to the country as a whole. A key tactic in that effort was to argue that the opening of the Panama Canal, a few years earlier, had changed the economy of the whole Mississippi Valley, meaning that "the trade centers of the Valley could regain the advantage only through the use of the low-cost transportation by inland waterways." [17]

Yet another line of argument, though, is the one that ultimately seems to have been the most effective, although it would later prove to be tragically ironic. Their coveted Tidewater Canal would one day have dire implications for the safety of New Orleans, particularly in the face of Katrina, but during the 1940s and 1950s, perhaps the key theme in the sales pitches from backers of the canal had to do with "security."

During World War II, part of the argument for the new canal involved the claim that the entire nation's productivity and output might suffer if an enemy were to attack New Orleans, creating a bottleneck at the bottom of the river. More than a decade later, Tidewater Canal proponents would argue that then-ongoing work on the St. Lawrence Seaway, connecting the Great Lakes to the Atlantic Ocean by way of Montreal, would also threaten national interests by drawing Midwestern trade with Europe through Canadian ports, and away from the "all-American" Mississippi River. In the intervening years, these arguments were supplemented with the claim that a second "outlet" for shipping would reduce the vulnerability of Mississippi River traffic to the kind of nuclear attack that might otherwise somehow "close the Mississippi River." The Mississippi, of course, has often demonstrated a basically irresistible ability to carve new channels when the old ones were closed up—that is, after all, how southern Louisiana came into existence in the first place—but the active and persistent partisans of the canal were not about to be stymied by such inconvenient details. In politics, after all, persistence can be more important than facts or logical consistency.

The next step was to seek support from the state's congressional delegation. This may have been the easiest of their tasks; they seem to have had little difficulty in convincing their senators and congressional representatives that it would be fine public policy to bring millions of federal dollars to the state. In short order, thanks in part to the urging of Colonel Alexander and the other members of the New Orleans Tidewater Development Association, the congressional representative from Louisiana's Sixth District—Henry D. Larcade Jr., who happened to be chair of the House Subcommittee on Rivers and Harbors—announced that he would seek authorization for the proposed seaway. In April and May of 1943, both the Commerce Committee of the U.S. Senate and Representative Larcade's Committee of the House directed the Corps of Engineers to study "the advisability and cost of providing an emergency outlet from the Mississippi River in the interest of national defense and general commerce."[18]

Much of the Army's attention was otherwise engaged at the time, given that the country was in the midst of World War II, so the study had to wait a few years. After the war, however, in May of 1948, the Chief of Engineers for the Army did finally endorse the idea of a new canal that would stretch from the Industrial Canal, in New Orleans, all the way to the Gulf of Mexico. By this time, the Corps appeared to agree with the arguments regarding "national security":

> The recent war demonstrated that harbor facilities, if dispersed and provided unrestricted access to the sea, are rendered inoperative by air or sea action with great difficulty.... Hence wide dispersion of harbor facilities should be provided for in any plan for comprehensive port development. New Orleans' riverside wharves, of timber construction on long wood piles, cannot be expected to resist destruction by bombing as practiced in the recent war, and attack by atom bomb now possible ... so preferably additional installations in the interest of national defense should be located off the river with an unrestricted outlet to the sea and access to the river through locks which from a security standpoint, can be considered as alternative entrances.[19]

Even with this endorsement of the national security argument, the Chief of Engineers was still somewhat limited in his enthusiasm at that time, but the governor of Louisiana was not. The man in question was the state's "singing governor," Jimmie Davis—whose other distinctive accomplishments include having written the song, "You Are My Sunshine"—and he wasted no time in singing the praises of this project, proclaiming that the new canal would be of "inestimable benefit" to the state and nation. Still, however "inestimable" the benefits might have seemed to Governor Davis, the Corps of Engineers was only allowed to consider "estimable" benefits, which the law required the agency to weigh against the costs of building the new project.[20]

Those estimates were eventually completed in the form of the official Benefit-Cost Analysis (BCA) that the agency forwarded to Congress in 1951. The BCA concluded that construction would cost just over $66 million (in 1948 dollars), with "corresponding annual carrying charges" of $4,027,000, including precisely $1,000,000 for maintenance expenses. Meanwhile, the BCA concluded that "the prospective tangible annual benefits" of building the new project would total $5,835,000. Those numbers amounted to good news for the project's boosters, because they translated into a positive net benefit-cost ratio of 1.45 to 1.[21]

The calculation of benefit-cost ratios can seem to be a highly complex and highly technical endeavor, but at its heart, the process

reflects a simple requirement. The *total* of all the benefits from building a water project must be found by the Corps to add up to more
than the number of *taxpayer* dollars going into the costs of building
it. In practice, however, the specific numbers can prove on closer
examination to be a kind of statistical smoke, swirling around a set
of judgments that are often inherently subjective. Additional issues
are raised by the fact that the dollars come from the entire nation's
taxpayers, while the benefits often go primarily to a small circle of
politically connected contractors and marine interests—a fact that
tends to be swept away in great rhetorical reveries about building
"the whole economy."

In the words of a noted critic, Ida Hoos,

> The cost-benefit exercise is usually a drunkard's search for data to
> support a given course of action. The frequency of benefit-to-cost
> ratios over one would surprise no one; the typical practice is to have
> advocates gather the data.... Data selection is by its nature an eclectic
> process. Substantiating data will be sought and used; data, once pli-
> able, become hardened through handling.[22]

One way to clarify the implications of benefit-cost requirements
is to think not in terms of building a dam or a canal, but in terms of
a welfare check. In simple calculations, welfare checks would almost
certainly have positive benefit-to-cost ratios: the recipient will typi-
cally spend the whole check—therefore, by definition, receiving
"economic benefits" that amount to the number on the face of the
check—but that is just the start. The widespread practice is for economic models to include "multipliers," representing the fact that, for
example, when some of the money is spent in a local grocery store,
the store will in turn spend some of that money to pay its employees,
who in turn will plow that income back into purchases of their own,
thus "multiplying" the total of the economic activity that will be set
in motion when new dollars are first added to an economy.

Debates over the issuance of welfare checks, however, rarely seem
to stop with such straightforward considerations. On one side of the
debate, partisans will argue that there are additional, intangible benefits that accrue to society, such as knowing that the welfare checks
can keep people from starving—meaning that the benefits are greater
than previously recognized or calculated. Partisans on the other side

of the debate will argue that, to the contrary, welfare checks create grave societal costs because welfare recipients might otherwise be looking for jobs, which would allow them to earn increased self-respect as well as regular paychecks, and thus that a "true" benefit-cost analysis would need to calculate the deeper costs that are incurred when welfare recipients are made to feel dependent and helpless—costs that, at least in the eyes of those critics, loom far larger than the direct dollar benefits represented by the monetary size of the checks alone. Through arguments such as this, the debates and the calculations can ramp up considerably—with the increasingly "technical" appearance of the arguments often ironically masking the fact that the discussions are in fact becoming increasingly subjective with each new layer of calculations.

A similar process has long been built into the debates over the costs and benefits of proposed pork-barrel projects—including but not limited to water projects—but with two contrasts that are particularly striking. First, in deliberations over such proposals, most partisans are relatively quick to set aside the recognition that the numbers in the debates are often just technical-looking guesses about actual dollar values. Second, the key partisans in these debates will rarely acknowledge that, in practice, they are often lobbying for welfare checks of their own.

In the most straightforward terms, the estimated benefit-cost ratio of 1.45 to 1 meant the Corps expected that the Mississippi River–Gulf Outlet would ultimately add $1.45 to the economy for every $1 of taxpayers' money—mainly from outside of the region—that would initially be invested in building the project. Over half of the anticipated benefits—an estimated $3.25 million out of a total of $5.84 million per year—were expected to come from a reduction of ship turnaround time. Another $950,000 worth of annual benefits were expected to come from "relief of congestion" at existing wharves and cargo terminals. Most of the rest was associated with the fact that, since MRGO was to be shorter and straighter than the Mississippi River's course from New Orleans to the Gulf—roughly 75 miles instead of 120—total shipping time and thus shipping costs should be reduced. Disappointing local boosters to some degree, the BCA concluded that MRGO should not be expected to benefit the region's petroleum industry, which was growing rapidly at the time, given the industry's "aversion to locks and side channels." Local agitation about the "fog-covered, silt-bearing, temperamental river channel" also appeared to have had little influence: The BCA noted that direct observations found only 14 hours per year of dense fog, "indicating that fog is only a minor navigation hazard for traffic to and from New Orleans."[23]

Working in the favor of local boosters, however, was one technicality with an importance that would grow considerably over time. The Dock Board, which was heavily involved in promoting the project, had previously submitted to the Chief of Engineers an estimate that the new channel would require an additional $1.38 million each year "for maintenance of the proposed channel," but the final BCA assessment estimated that the total of all maintenance costs—including but not limited to the ongoing dredging—would amount to just $1 million per year. All other costs of maintenance dredging basically disappeared from the "annual" comparison of costs versus benefits. That omission is all the more remarkable in that other Dock Board estimates appear to have been far too low. The Dock Board's estimate of construction costs, for example, was just $25 million—well under half of the $66 million figure used in the final BCA and a significantly smaller fraction of the actual construction costs that would become evident later.

The disappearance of much of the ongoing maintenance cost from the analysis would have fundamental consequences. MRGO was excavated through the heart of a profoundly fragile and unstable environment. As will be spelled out in subsequent chapters, the ongoing ordeal of MRGO maintenance dredging would mean increasing costs to the environment as well as to U.S. taxpayers. By the time Katrina hit New Orleans, the annual maintenance dredging would be costing $15–25 million per year—to say nothing of the incalculable environmental costs to the wetlands that had done so much to protect New Orleans up to that time. Still, the ongoing expenditures for dredging did prove useful in creating yet another interest group for the ongoing maintenance of MRGO, namely the dredging industry.

A "Helpful Explosion for World Trade"?

If the Chief of Engineers had been less effusive about MRGO than Louisiana's rapturous Governor Davis, the acting director of the Bureau of the Budget, Elmer Statts, responded to the benefit-cost analysis with even less enthusiasm, concluding that the project's cost could not be justified in terms of "direct monetary benefits from the outlet channel to the Gulf." On the other hand, he noted that the plan also called for an expansion of the "inner harbor" along the Industrial Canal. For Director Statts, it was this new harbor space, coupled with the proposed "future construction" of a new lock on the Mississippi River—intended to bring river traffic to the new harbor, bypassing the rapidly aging Industrial Canal lock—that could tip the balance in favor of the project. All in all, he concluded, there would be enough "advantages of convenience and efficiency" from combining MRGO with a harbor improvement project that he would have "no objection" to the authorization of the project, "with the understanding, however, that no appropriation for construction of the project will be sought until such time as the budgetary situation clearly makes possible the initiation of such improvements."[24]

Had Statts been more careful, he might have indicated that "no appropriation for construction of the project [would] be sought" *by his office*. Local boosters and the Louisiana congressional delegation, on the other hand, had been pushing this project for more than a quarter of a century by this time, and they were under no such constraint.

For several years, proposals for funding had been blocked in Congress, perhaps in part because "upper Mississippi Valley supporters of the Louisiana seaway were more interested in the St. Lawrence seaway, which New Orleans opposed, and withdrew their votes until the St. Lawrence project had passed Congress. After congressional approval of the St. Lawrence seaway in 1954, opposition to the New Orleans project faded." Accordingly, it may not have been a coincidence that the time when local persistence paid off came reasonably soon after the approval of the St. Lawrence seaway. Just two years later, the River and Harbors Act of 1956 officially authorized the construction of the canal, being signed into law by President Eisenhower on March 29, 1956—but without any provisions for the new lock.[25]

Even at that point, the boosters continued to show ingenuity and persistence. Although the common pattern at the time was for such "authorized" projects to wait for years before receiving actual congressional "appropriations" or funding, the Dock Board itself soon used $200,000, advanced from the New Orleans Levee Board, to initiate construction. On December 10, 1957, the construction started with a literal bang—from 180 sticks of dynamite, which created what the *New Orleans Times-Picayune* would call a "helpful explosion for world trade"—cheered on by about a hundred businessmen and officials as well as a supportive press corps.[26]

This "helpful explosion for world trade" actually amounted to a trivially small fraction of the overall cost of the project, which would ultimately run thousands of times that high, to a total of $580 million—with many of those millions being dollars from the 1950s and 1960s. The explosion was certainly "helpful," however, as a public-relations stunt and as a way of energizing the local effort to bring in the needed federal funding. The Corps began its own work on MRGO a few months later, in March 1958.[27]

The first explosion of criticism about the environmental and social costs of MRGO came at about the same time. In the era before the first "Earth Day" in 1970, water projects were seldom opposed with any great vigor or effect. Yet even in the 1950s and 1960s—almost fifty years before Katrina, and beginning nearly a decade before Hurricane Betsy hit New Orleans in 1965—scientists and wildlife managers expressed clear concerns, arguing that the risks of MRGO were too great to overlook. Opponents to the project, both locally and nationally, may have had far fewer resources than the project's backers, politically or economically, but they were equally determined—and in retrospect, they appear to have been far more accurate in their expectations.

Over half a year before the "helpful explosion," and even longer before the actual excavation by the Corps got under way in earnest, a "Statement of Concern" from the Louisiana Wildlife and Fisheries Commission provided clear evidence of the economic as well as environmental significance of "highly valuable and irreplaceable fish and wildlife resources and areas" that appeared likely to be affected by the project—characterized by the commission as "the most important area in southeast Louisiana" except for the Mississippi River Delta itself. Perhaps in response to the benefit-cost assessment by the Corps, the commission went beyond overall statements of concern, providing some economic numbers of its own—numbers that appear to have been much "harder" or closer to actual market values than were many of the figures used by the Corps.

More specifically, the commission noted that shrimp harvests in the area affected by MRGO were "carefully estimated as being worth $20 million annually," and that the oysters and wetland areas east of the Mississippi River had an estimated value of an additional $4 million annually. The commission added that "the loss of this marsh as a waterfowl area cannot be compensated for elsewhere," but that in cases where marsh development had been possible, the development costs had exceeded $300 per acre, in 1950s dollars—plus land acquisition costs, plus annual maintenance costs of another 10 percent— pointing to an implied cost of another $15 million even if it were physically possible to develop marshlands comparable in quality to those threatened by MRGO.[28]

In light of the fact that the officially estimated *total* cost of MRGO was expected by the Corps to be just $66 million, adding in even these simple estimates of replacement costs for the wetlands would have increased the cost of the project significantly—despite the optimistic estimates that were used elsewhere in the official benefit-cost analysis. Indeed, as just noted, the official BCA from the Corps had concluded that "the prospective tangible annual benefits" of building the new project would total $5,835,000. Including as little as a quarter of the Wildlife and Fisheries Commission's estimate of the potential loss of shrimp and oyster harvests ($6 million per year, or one quarter of the estimated $24 million per year) would have turned the entire balance between benefits and costs in the negative direction—*even if the estimated construction cost had been zero.*

The concerns of local wildlife managers were even echoed in the nation's capital. Also in 1957, before the start of any excavation, Fred Seaton, the U.S. Secretary of the Interior, wrote a letter to the Secretary of the Army, Wilbur M. Brucker, asking him to proceed slowly with the project. Seaton's letter cited fears that the dredging operation could destroy estuaries that formed the backbone of local shrimp, oyster, and fishing industries, as well as degrading the region's marshes.[29]

Several months later—roughly a year after the Statement of Concern from the Louisiana Wildlife and Fisheries Commission, or about the time when the Corps was beginning the excavation— a more extensive report from the Department of the Interior effectively endorsed the views of the Louisiana wildlife managers. This "interim report" from the department (we have been unable to find a "final" report) concluded that the marshes through which MRGO would be carved were indeed highly valuable, and that excavation of MRGO "could result in major ecological change of the area," creating "widespread and severe consequences." The federal report concurred with the judgment that these specific marshes constituted "by far the most important waterfowl area in southeast Louisiana" outside of the Mississippi River Delta itself. As the report noted, these marshes were the source of about 20 percent of all the fish and shellfish of Louisiana—if not more, given their role as a nursery for species such as shrimp that were ultimately harvested in other locations. Overall, the federal report decreed this stretch of marshes to be characterized by an "inconceivably large supply of living plants and animal organisms.... These in the aggregate constitute perhaps the densest and richest wild fauna in the world."[30]

Wildlife managers were not the only ones to raise concerns. The controversy was particularly noteworthy in St. Bernard Parish, which lies immediately to the east of New Orleans, adjacent to the lower Ninth Ward, and which contains most of the territory that MRGO traverses.

St. Bernard Parish had long been home to a certain skepticism toward water-related projects intended to benefit New Orleans; it was in St. Bernard Parish, after all, that levees had been dynamited during the great Mississippi River floods of 1927, with the theory being that this invitation for the river to flood St. Bernard Parish would take pressure off the New Orleans levees. Particularly notable, however, were the warnings from the then-owner of the local newspaper, the *St. Bernard Voice*, Edwin M. Roy, the second generation of the Roy family to own and edit the newspaper. Although St. Bernard Parish would be heavily damaged by Hurricane Katrina, nearly fifty years later, the *Voice* would survive even that challenge, continuing to be published under the third-generation Ed Roy.

Unlike the *Times-Picayune* of neighboring New Orleans—which at the time provided a skepticism-free zone for local Growth Machine efforts to promote MRGO—Roy's *Voice* ran a series of outspokenly critical editorials, with some of the most notable examples running just before and after the ground-breaking ceremony for the project on December 10, 1957. Roy's words were anything but meek. Through the months of November and December of 1957, the editorials ran at the top of page one of the weekly issues, all under uppercase headlines asking, "IS ST. BERNARD PARISH DOOMED?"

Clearly, Edwin Roy was no enemy of economic growth; instead, he was concerned about what MRGO would mean for the future of St. Bernard Parish. He noted, for example, that the parish on the opposite side of New Orleans, Jefferson, was experiencing much more rapid growth at the time than was St. Bernard parish, even though "St. Bernard Parish should be enjoying and have the same position in the State of Louisiana, in growth, as Jefferson Parish." His arguments, incidentally, have a certain plausibility: New Orleans itself was to reach its highest census population just a few years later—640,000 persons, in 1960—and at the time, population growth was spreading past the city's boundaries, creating the kinds of rapid suburbanization and sprawl in nearby jurisdictions that were also being seen around other U.S. cities by the middle years of the twentieth century.[31]

Some of Roy's key concerns involved the fact that St. Bernard Parish was already on the wrong side of the channels and the region's economic equations, and so he saw reasons to worry that MRGO might well make matters worse. Where the New Orleans *Times-Picayune* saw a "helpful explosion for world trade," accordingly, he saw a looming threat, warning his readers that "Residents of St. Bernard Parish had better become conscious of the Tidewater Channel. It certainly will affect every resident of this parish in some manner."[32]

In fact, some of his editorials focused on the very roadways and bridges from which later generations would observe the ever-spreading effects of MRGO. One of the potential problems that worried him appears in retrospect not to have materialized, namely that MRGO—like the Industrial Canal, which by that time had been in operation for several decades—would generate long waits for traffic at local bridges, thereby impeding parish growth. In his concerns about MRGO's likely environmental impact, however, Roy appears to have been prescient. He was worried that many of the parish's economic activities were directly dependent on the region's natural resources, and a number of the editorials raised environmental concerns that would grow considerably in significance throughout the decades to come.

In an editorial that ran just before the MRGO ground-breaking, for example, he warned that "Shell Beach, a well-known fishing resort, will no longer be accessible to the public by automobile"—a prediction that later proved to be correct. The same editorial asked just how much "the Tidewater Channel" would affect "other fishing grounds in St. Bernard Parish where many thousands of people fish the year round," along with "the oyster and shrimp industry of the parish." The editorial went on to ask, "How about hunting and trapping? These are questions the residents of St. Bernard Parish, especially those in the lower section of the parish who make their living off fishing and trapping, should know. None of the answers have been forthcoming."[33]

The following week, just after the official ground-breaking, Roy's editorial was still more prophetic:

> St. Bernard Parish comprises roughly an area of 635 square miles, most of which, of course, is marsh land. When the Tidewater Channel is cut through the parish, approximately 335 square miles of St. Bernard Parish will be on the "outside" of the channel. Will it disappear forever in a few years after the channel is completed?
>
> A committee appointed by the present police jury [a board equivalent to a county commission in most states] is presently seeking information and will soon make a report and recommendations to that august body.[34]

Evidently, when "that august body" got the information it requested, it wound up agreeing with the editorials in *St. Bernard Voice*. The Police Jury not only began an investigation and held public meetings on the questions that Roy and others were asking, but a few months later, in April 1958, the St. Bernard Parish Police Jury officially reversed its earlier statement of support for the project.[35]

At that time, the MRGO was still in its very first month of construction, meaning that the vast majority of future damage might well have been avoided if the construction had simply stopped then. After decades of dogged lobbying, however, none of the project's most influential backers in the region were in any mood to pull the plug, and neither was the U.S. Army Corps of Engineers. Instead, as the construction crews carved their way though the wetlands, the controversy—and the environmental damage—continued to grow.

Chapter 6

The Collapse of
Engineered Systems

Y 1963, a narrow preliminary channel of MRGO had been excavated all the way to the Gulf of Mexico, allowing a ship named the *Del Sud* to make the first trip along the canal's full length. The entire project was officially declared complete five years later, or a decade after construction started, in 1968. If any one event could be said to have crystallized and broadened local concerns about MRGO, that event would have come near the midpoint between the first vessel and the official completion, when Hurricane Betsy slammed ashore in 1965. The storm created a much higher level of flooding than had been expected, and it first gave MRGO the nickname of "the hurricane highway."[1]

For the record, the Army Corps of Engineers disagreed with criticism of "the hurricane highway" at the time, and it still does. In the eyes of many locals, on the other hand, the Corps has reason to be defensive. Aside from FEMA and the larger Department of Homeland Security, no other federal agency came in for so much criticism in the aftermath of Katrina as the U.S. Army Corps of Engineers. Much of the reason for that criticism involves the fact that the Corps built the levees and floodwalls that failed to protect the city. Still, just as a ship can sink because of a single hole, most of the damage to New

Orleans came from the floodwalls along just three specific canals—the London Avenue, 17th Street, and Industrial Canals. We have already discussed the initial construction of the Industrial Canal, and we will soon examine that canal's role in the flooding in greater detail, but first, it is worth considering the other two.

Colleagues who are not from New Orleans have seen maps of the drainage canals and wondered why in the world anyone would dig canals into the heart of a low-lying city. The short answer is, no one did. The London Avenue and 17th Street canals—both of which were initially intended to drain water out of the city, not to bring it in—were excavated through the swamps at a time when no one expected that the area they traversed would ever become part of the city. The full answer is only slightly longer.

Some of the underlying story can be seen by comparing an old map of New Orleans, which was drawn to show the flooding caused by a crevasse (breach) on the Mississippi River levee in 1849, against a much more recent satellite photo of Katrina's flooding. As can be seen, despite the fact that more than a century and a half passed between the two floods, the inundated areas show a strikingly similar pattern. The key difference is that, at the time of the earlier map—even though it dates from a century and a half or so after the founding of New Orleans—there was still very little development except on top of the natural levee, hugging the banks of the Mississippi River.

There were good reasons why settlement clung so carefully to the area along the river's banks: as noted earlier, the natural levees along the banks of the river provided the only "high" ground in the region, with the elevation becoming lower and the soils becoming increasingly soggy as distance from the river increased. Until very recently, there was virtually no development north of the Metairie and Gentilly Ridges—the curving lines in the older map, about midway between the river and the lake—and in fact, many of the fine homes that a current visitor to New Orleans can observe along St. Charles Avenue were built from cypress trees that were harvested out of the swamps between those ridges and Lake Pontchartrain.

It was not until the early twentieth century, after a new kind of heavy-duty pump was designed by A. Baldwin Wood—a gifted engineer who later became director of the city's Sewerage and Water

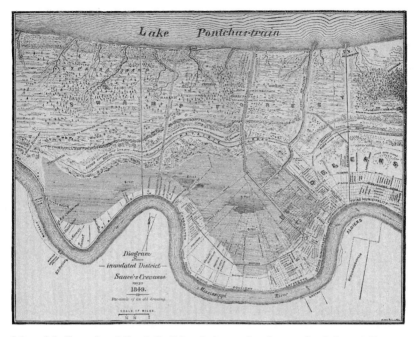

Map of the "inundated district" of New Orleans after the 1849 flood through "Sauvé's Crevasse." Shading indicates flooded areas; Metarie and Gentilly "ridges" are visible roughly midway between the Mississippi River and Lake Pontchartrain. Note location of drainage canals, top, plus the fact that the natural levee along the Mississippi River, near the bottom, did not flood.

Board—that it became possible to "improve" the city's drainage. Still, even at the time when the canals were being dug through the two ridges, and when pumps were being placed on the north side of those ridges, it seems not to have occurred to engineers, or to almost anyone else, that homes might some day be built in the swamps through which the canals were being excavated.

In the late 1920s, however, as part of an effort to create a barrier against storm surges from Lake Pontchartrain that could threaten the north side of the city, officials dredged the lake to create a narrow strip of elevated land along the lakefront, which is visible as a narrow strip of dry (lighter-color) ground near the top of the satellite photo. By adding this higher "lip" along the lake's shore, unfortunately, the dredging also created a bowl between the natural levee of the

New Orleans area in 2005, showing flooding from Hurricane Katrina (darker areas). The French Quarter is located just to the right of the center of the photo, on the northwest side of the sharp bend in the Mississippi River, across from what locals know as Algiers Point. Photograph courtesy of SPOT at the University of California, Santa Barbara, © CNES 2007, Distributed by Terra Image USA, LLC and SPOT IMAGE.

Mississippi and the lake. As pumping technology continued to improve, it became possible to drain this bowl.

Nature may or may not abhor a vacuum, but real estate speculators often do—particularly when the "vacuum" involves major expanses of flat, "empty" land, right next to a growing city. Over the same decades of the twentieth century when so many other U.S. cities were also experiencing considerable sprawl, virtually all of the swampland in that bowl was turned into urban neighborhoods. Unfortunately, rather than filling in the drainage canals—which after all had been doing their intended job for many decades by that time—officials left the canals where they were, adding levees and floodwalls to keep the water away from the new housing developments. Among these were the floodwalls along the London Avenue and 17th Street canals.

A further complication was introduced by the fact that the soil associated with these former swamps was rich in organic material. When this soil dried out, it settled—and the organic material began to decay as it came into contact with oxygen, causing the land to sink, or subside, even more. In short, the new neighborhoods, while generally dry, at least as long as the pumps could be counted on, were clearly not "high." Many were in fact well below sea level, and sinking, protected from flooding only by the levees, floodwalls, and pumps—at least until the arrival of Katrina.

The First Clue: When Is Water Not Level?

After Katrina, as noted in the early pages of this book, the Corps did acknowledge that its "system" of flood protection structures "did not perform as a system." Like a chain, after all, a flood protection system can be only as strong as its weakest link. One important problem is that—contrary to early reports—many of the failures occurred when water levels were well below what the floodwalls were supposed to have been able to handle. Another telling clue, however, is that floodwaters in other areas were significantly deeper.

In fairness, it should be noted that the Corps originally wanted levees instead of floodwalls, agreeing to build floodwalls only after local opposition prevented the construction of levees. The basic difference is that levees are built of soil and have a broad base and cross-section, often hundreds of feet across. This makes them much stronger than the floodwalls in New Orleans, which look like ordinary concrete walls, except that they sit on top of corrugated steel "sheet" pilings—designed to interlock with adjoining pilings—that were driven down into the soft soil underneath. The reason for the opposition was that the broader base of a levee requires a much larger footprint than does a floodwall, eating into the land that might otherwise have been made available for real-estate development—as well as taking over the backyards or even the homes in adjacent neighborhoods. Although the Corps is often accused of not listening to local input, it was precisely because of local preferences that the Corps decided to build floodwalls instead of levees in this case.[2]

Yet that is only one part of the story. The current estimate from the

Water flowing slowly out of 17th Street Canal, August 30, 2005. Note that water levels barely reach the bottom of the concrete portions of the wall, roughly eight feet below the top of the wall. Photograph by Nathan Bassiouni.

Corps is that roughly 67 percent of the flooding came from design flaws in the levees and floodwalls. The National Science Foundation's Independent Levee Investigation Team (2006) came up with estimates in the range of 75–80 percent or higher. This minor difference in percentage estimates is less significant than the fact that, according to both assessments, floodwaters never came close to the tops of two of the floodwalls just mentioned—the 17th Street and London Avenue canals. Along the third, by contrast—the Industrial Canal—the water was enough higher that it poured right over the top of the floodwalls, even though the walls along all three canals were theoretically parts of the same system.[3]

That difference, in fact, may offer an important clue—one that should set off warning lights not just for professional hydrologists but for anyone who has ever taken a high-school physics class, or for that matter, for any small child who has ever built dams and ponds along a mud puddle or a beach. All three of the most important

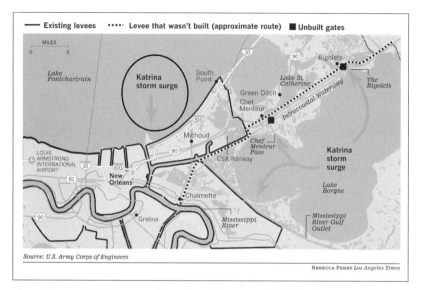

Army Corps of Engineers explanation of the source of the flooding, as published in the Los Angeles Times *(accompanying Vartabedian and Pae, 2005). This was the report of the breaches near the "throat of the funnel" that will be discussed in the next chapter (it is located at the center of this figure, with the "top" pointing right). Note the claim that the flooding came from Lake Pontchartrain, to the north, meaning the city could have been protected if environmental opposition had not prevented the Corps from building a barrier that would have stopped the storm surge from getting into Lake Pontchartrain. Note also that this map includes no indication of any storm surge coming into or through the funnel. Image © Copyright 2005 Los Angeles Times, Graphic by Rebecca Perry. Reprinted with permission.*

floodwall failures—those along the London Avenue, 17th Street, and Industrial canals—took place where the floodwalls were built to roughly the same height, and all three canals connect to the same Lake Pontchartrain. If the main source of flooding for New Orleans had been the rising water of Lake Pontchartrain, to the north of the city—which is what the Corps of Engineers originally claimed—then the water levels in all three of the canals should have been basically the same. That was clearly not the case.[4]

The differences, moreover, were anything but small. Specific estimates do vary, but the floodwaters that reached the Industrial Canal appear to have been 5–8 feet higher than those in the other two canals. Calculations by the LSU Hurricane Center—but also by the Corps of Engineers—concluded that the storm surges that affected the Industrial Canal and thus the Lower Ninth Ward were 15–18 feet high, while the surges that affected the 17th Street and London Avenue canals, flooding the areas of New Orleans to the west of the Industrial Canal, were in the range of 10–12 feet. That, of course, simply would not have happened if the heaviest flooding had indeed come in from Lake Pontchartrain, as the Corps of Engineers originally claimed.[5]

That difference also proved to be no minor distinction for the human lives involved. Along the 17th Street and London Avenue canals, the floodwaters coming through the breaches and gaps rose relatively slowly, which is one of the reasons why so many observers initially thought that the floodwalls had held. One resident interviewed by the *Times-Picayune* measured the rising floodwaters by bricks: initially, just the street was wet, but eventually he noticed that the waters were rising, doing so at a rate of about one brick per hour. Another resident—Gaynel Gassert, one of the lab technicians at Tulane Hospital, which stayed out of the headlines largely because the staff and management did such an effective job of evacuating sick patients—took photos of the streets outside the hospital, first during the day on Monday and then at sunrise on Tuesday, showing streets that were merely wet the first day and clearly under water the next day.[6]

The experience was terrifyingly different on the other side of the Industrial Canal. There—in the Lower Ninth Ward and in adjacent St. Bernard Parish—residents who until that moment had trusted the flood "protection" from the Corps of Engineers were attacked by a veritable wall of water, bursting through the Industrial Canal floodwalls as well as the MRGO levees, surging over the tops of their roofs, with some houses being inundated or even flattened, sometimes in a matter of seconds.

The reason for the difference is that, in the Lower Ninth Ward, the water came pouring over the top of the Industrial Canal floodwall, carving a ditch or "scour" in the soft soil behind the wall. Soon, rather than having about fourteen feet of dirt to support the additional eight feet or so of the wall that had formerly extended above the soil, the ditch became so deep that only about the bottom eight feet of the

Views of the corner of Canal and Treme, as seen from the Windows of Tulane Hospital, August 29 (above) and 30 (below), 2005. Photographs by Gaynel Gassert.

corrugated "sheet" pilings were still backed by anything more solid than air or water—while the raging waters from the canal side were putting ever-increasing leverage on the top of the wall.

In effect, the removal of the soil created a contest between an irresistible force and what proved to be a distinctly moveable object. The floodwall, still connected to the sheet pilings, was shoved to the east by the still-rising waters. It scraped across a broad swath of the

Remaining portion of Industrial Canal floodwall, October 9, 2005. Note that water had clearly come over the top of the wall, carving away the soil on the "back" side of the wall (facing the Lower Ninth Ward). Near the top of the photo is the portion of the wall that gave way catastrophically—the location from which the photo on page 101 was taken. Photograph by William Freudenburg.

adjoining neighborhood, the Lower Ninth Ward, shoving away the homes like a battalion of bulldozers. Once the interlocking joints of the pilings ruptured and the wall toppled, the wall of water behind it burst out to do even greater damage. Some sections of the floodwall ultimately ended up flattened out across former home sites, more than 170 feet to the east of where they had been expected to remain standing.

Up until the instant when the floodwall on the east side of the Industrial Canal failed so catastrophically, the Lower Ninth Ward had been a densely settled urban neighborhood of historic one-story homes, populated predominantly by black residents, and character-ized by high levels of home ownership. In that instant, however, the floodwaters suddenly rose past the levels where the rooftops had stood only moments before, and the neighborhood became one with

Flattened portion of Industrial Canal floodwall, which had been shoved more than 170 feet into the Lower Ninth Ward, as it looked on October 9, 2005. Interlocking segments of the corrugated steel sheet piling are in the foreground, to the left of the flattened wall. Remaining pieces of the concrete portion of the wall, which formerly stood above ground, lie to right. This was once a densely populated urban neighborhood. The photo was taken with a telephoto lens; the one remaining home near the top center of the photograph was four to five blocks away from the breach. Houses within four to six blocks of the floodwall were completely swept away, and many of those within the next several blocks were effectively destroyed as well. Photograph by Robert Gramling.

high levels of homelessness, instead. For a stretch of some four blocks from the floodwall breach, every single house was scraped off its foundations—often leaving no trace, not even a cinderblock. In other cases, the only reminder of the previous existence of a home would be a portion of a sidewalk, or the remnants of a concrete slab, with all but the last few of the linoleum tiles having been torn off by the torrent. The debris—cars and trucks, roofs and walls, baby carriages and bathroom fixtures, and much more—were deposited at least four to six city blocks farther into the neighborhood.

"Dead truck," which had been overturned by floodwaters before having a house wind up on top of it. This house, in turn, had been shoved to this location by another house that was also carried by the raging floodwaters. This image gives some idea of the level of damage that was still present in the Lower Ninth Ward, roughly five blocks from the main breach, more than six months after the storm. Photograph by Robert Gramling.

Given that many of the local citizens had believed the official assurances that the floodwalls would protect them—and given that hurricane-strength winds and rainfall were howling just outside—many of them tried to "escape" by climbing higher inside their homes. Some climbed on tops of cabinets or dressers; others made their way into their attics. So fast and so high did the waters rise, however, that many who stayed in their houses would never again be seen alive.

Some portions of those houses would never be seen again, either. Other portions—a roof here, a refrigerator there, an overturned pickup truck still farther away—would be scattered in a grotesquely random fashion, where they would lie without being further disturbed for months or even years after the storm. Yet another dozen blocks into the neighborhood, a larger number of houses managed to

A makeshift shrine—a teddy bear in a child's "life preserver," or personal flotation device. The shrine was in a house in the Lower Ninth Ward that had been destroyed by Katrina, roughly six blocks from the main breach and more than six months after the storm. Photograph by William Freudenburg.

withstand the floodwaters—some of them well enough that kitchen clocks were still attached to the walls. In one house there, we found a clock that stopped at 7:53 a.m. In the kitchen next door—perhaps because it was slightly higher off the floor, or perhaps because the owner had kept track of time a bit differently—the clock had stopped at 7:57. Both clocks provided silent but eloquent testimony that the people of the Lower Ninth Ward endured a very different type of experience than did those in most of New Orleans. A careful reconstruction of fatality data by researchers from the Netherlands found that citizens living close to the breach in the Lower Ninth Ward were five to seven times more likely to be killed by Katrina's flooding than were those who lived on the other side of the Industrial Canal.[7]

A difference that deadly, surely, merits a search for additional clues.

That is particularly true in light of the fact that additional clues are not so hard to find. Katrina, after all, was far from being the first major hurricane to hit New Orleans around the time of a Labor Day weekend. A pair of Katrina's predecessors happen to share that distinction, and both are worthy of a closer look.

The Second Clue: Other Stormy Weather

Students who study the scientific method learn early on about the value of laboratory experiments. In essence, they learn that the perfect experiment is one where observations can be identical except in one way. The classic example involves two test tubes: if outcomes are different in the test tube that contains some new ingredient, versus the one that doesn't, the logical conclusion is that the new ingredient accounts for the difference.

At some point in their studies, however, those same students are likely to learn that, in the real world, laboratory-style matches of this sort are very difficult to find. It would be impossible—both ethically and meteorologically—to create a pair of perfectly matched hurricanes and then slam them into two different sections of the coastline, or to have them both follow precisely the same track at different points in time. Every now and then, however, nature and chance will conspire to provide us with sets of circumstances that are sufficiently well matched to create what scientists call a "natural experiment." For comparisons to Katrina, we have not just one but two reasonably close matches—the famous storms named Hurricanes Betsy and Camille.

It was almost exactly forty years before Katrina, near the end of August 1965, when an earlier "tropical depression" or low-pressure system started to form in the warm waters to the southeast of Florida. The names of hurricanes are sometimes "retired," much like the jerseys of major sports stars, but only after particularly noteworthy storms. Thus it was that, when this weather system became a tropical storm, it was given a name that had also been used for far less damaging storms in 1956 and 1961—Betsy.

After spinning somewhat erratically in the Atlantic Ocean for several days, Betsy veered to the southwest, across the southern end of

Florida, subjecting Miami to hurricane-force winds for some twelve hours before roaring over the Florida Keys on September 7. At that point, the storm started picking up speed in two senses—soaking up enough energy from the warm waters of the Gulf of Mexico to become a major or Category 4 storm, with winds up to 155 mph, and also dispensing with its earlier pattern of erratic meandering, seemingly making up its mind instead to head straight toward New Orleans. To some observers, it seemed almost like a renewed sense of purpose in a shark that has just tasted blood—as if the storm had received so much of an adrenaline rush from doing a bit of damage to Florida that it became intent on doing some truly serious damage the next time it reached land. Just two days later, on September 9, 1965, Betsy ripped into the coastal regions to the south of New Orleans, doing so as a still-strong Category 3 storm. By the next day, Betsy had become the most expensive hurricane in U.S. history—at least at that time.[8]

Hurricane Betsy flooded some 164,000 homes and killed 76 people in Louisiana alone, in the process of causing an estimated $1.42 billion in damage. No previous storm had ever created as much as a billion dollars in damage, so the nickname of "Billion-Dollar Betsy" proved to be both obvious and irresistible. When adjusted for inflation, $1.42 billion in 1965 dollars would be the equivalent of $8.5 billion in 2000 dollars.

In a pattern that would become much better known some forty years later, many of the deaths occurred as residents drowned in their attics, trapped and unable to climb any higher to escape from the still-rising waters. Press photos from the time show scenes that seem eerily familiar from the perspective of the twenty-first century—cars in water up to their roofs, neighborhoods in water up to chest levels, citizens escaping in flat-bottomed boats. At first glance, it seems as though the main difference is the styling of the cars, or perhaps the fact that the earlier pictures are mainly black and white. On closer examination, though, probably the more telling difference for people who are familiar with the neighborhoods in question is that the flooding from Betsy was far less deep, and the damage was far less severe, than would be the case with Katrina forty years later.

Hurricane Camille came in four years after Betsy, on the night

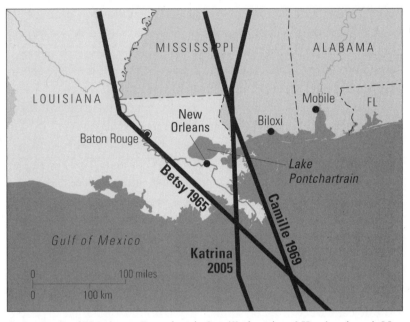

Storm tracks of Hurricanes Betsy (1965), Camille (1969) and Katrina (2005). Note that Betsy went just to the west of New Orleans, exposing the city to that storm's dangerous "right hook," while Camille and Katrina passed about the same distance to the east of the city. Storm track information from National Oceanic and Atmospheric Administration (NOAA); original cartography by Cliff Duplechin. Source: World Watch *Magazine, Vol. 20, No. 5, Sept./Oct. 2007, www.worldwatch.org.*

of August 17, 1969, blazing a path that was even closer to the route that Katrina would later follow. In comparing the three storms, it is worth remembering once again that the most destructive wind and water come from a hurricane's "right hook"—the front right quadrant of the storm's counterclockwise rotation, where wind speeds are increased by the hurricane's forward movement, and more important, where the winds are coming directly toward humans from across open water, driving the highest storm surges. Betsy went just to the west of New Orleans, hitting the city with that right hook, while both Camille and Katrina followed a track that was just to the east of the city, meaning that their most punishing winds and waters hit the Mississippi coastline instead, with flooding of New Orleans coming from the upper left or northwest side of the eye. Still, the paths of Camille and Katrina revealed the potential for storm surges to come from the east and southeast—and as will be spelled out in the next chapter, that may have become an increasingly vulnerable side of the city by the Katrina hit.

The eye of Camille barely grazed the Mississippi River Delta and then came ashore just a bit to the east, coming within less than a dozen miles of the spot that Katrina would later cross. Camille was also like Katrina in producing a terrifying storm surge—the largest ever seen at that time, variously estimated to have been 24–28 feet deep. A later report on Katrina from the National Hurricane Center would note an unofficial storm tide observation of 28 feet at the Emergency Operations Center in Hancock, Mississippi, "suggest[ing] that the storm surge produced by Katrina was as high as about 27 feet at that location," and some informal estimates indicated that Katrina's surge may have been even higher in a few locations to the east of the eye along the Mississippi Gulf Coast. Both Katrina and Camille were large storms, creating surges as far to the east as the panhandle of Florida, although Katrina was the largest of the three storms in terms of the total area covered by its winds. According to the record books, Katrina briefly reached a slightly greater intensity than did Camille while each storm was still over the Gulf of Mexico, but Camille was the stronger hurricane when it actually came ashore.[9]

In addition to wind speeds, the strength of hurricanes can also be measured in terms of the barometric pressure in the center or eye of the storm. Normal pressure at sea level is about a thousand millibars, or mbar (1013 mbar, to be precise). The faster a storm is turning—sucking wind toward the eye of the hurricane and then up, in a spinning version of a chimney effect—the lower the pressure, and the stronger the storm. Rather than weakening before hitting land, like Betsy and Katrina, Camille reached its strongest intensity just as it was coming ashore, with a near-record-low barometric pressure of 909 mbar. (For comparison purposes, Katrina came ashore with a pressure of 920 mbar.)

At the time of landfall, Camille's winds rose to a peak of at least 190 mph, possibly becoming the strongest wind speeds ever recorded in a hurricane, but there is no way to know for sure. Just before Camille pounded into the shores of Louisiana, an Air Force reconnaissance aircraft estimated that the winds might actually be blowing as hard as 205 mph, but with the winds blowing that hard, the crew was unable to produce a definitive measurement of the wind speed. Camille forced the last 125 miles of the Mississippi River to flow backward—meaning that the current was heading in the "wrong" direction past New Orleans—and it was backed up for an additional 120 miles, past Baton Rouge. With the possible exception of an unnamed Labor Day storm that hit Key West in 1935, Camille brought ashore the strongest winds of any hurricane ever recorded in the mainland United States.[10]

It is reasonable to assume that, if nothing else had changed during the interim, then the city that had weathered Betsy and Camille, both with higher wind speeds at impact, would be expected to survive even a larger Hurricane Katrina. That is particularly true in light of the fact that Betsy's damage to the New Orleans region in 1965 is what led to what the Army Corps of Engineers called the "The Hurricane Protection Program." That program built new levees and floodwalls that were both taller and stronger than those that had been in place up through the 1960s, being specifically designed to resist a fast-moving Category 3 hurricane like Betsy. Thus, in theory, Katrina should have created less devastation to the city, not only because the intensity was comparable or in some respects lower, but also because the later protection system was significantly more robust.

Unfortunately, whatever the hypothetical differences in potential between Katrina and the two comparison storms from the 1960s, Katrina's actual devastation was far worse. Both Camille and Betsy did create some flooding in New Orleans, with Betsy flooding about 20 percent of the homes in the city. Katrina, on the other hand, flooded 80 percent of New Orleans, leaving parts of the city submerged under more than a dozen feet of water. Camille killed 143 people along the Gulf coast, many of them in Mississippi, while Betsy proved to be deadlier for New Orleans and Louisiana, killing a total of 76 Louisiana residents. Katrina, on the other hand, killed about twenty times as many of the state's residents.

To repeat, this "natural experiment," like most, is inherently partial and imperfect. In particular, Katrina's larger size created the potential for high storm surges, particularly to the east of the eye, along the Mississippi coastline. Still, it is clear that something else—some important variable—must have changed between 1965 and 2005. Given that geological changes take place only quite slowly, then a reasonable guess would be that any changes taking place in just a few decades probably had something to do with human influences. Of all the human-influenced changes that took place in the region during those decades, it would be hard to imagine any that were more important than the loss of the region's protective wetlands.

Chapter 7

The Loss of
Natural Defenses

*E*VEN BEFORE Katrina's floodwaters had drained away, the investigations had begun. One of the patterns to emerge from those investigations is that the U.S. Army Corps of Engineers continues to disagree, strongly, with the critics of MRGO—meaning that the agency's officials, at least, would almost certainly disagree with almost everything in this chapter. In the interest of fairness, accordingly, we will turn first to the official views of the Corps before summarizing the ways in which independent experts—and affected citizens—view the relevant evidence.

The post-Katrina version of the official position of the Corps is spelled out in a hefty volume with a correspondingly hefty name— *Performance Evaluation of the New Orleans and Southeast Louisiana Hurricane Protection System: Draft Final Report of the Interagency Performance Evaluation Task Force*. In that report and elsewhere, the Corps does acknowledge that many of its levees failed, but the agency's official position is that the Mississippi River–Gulf Outlet had virtually nothing to do with the death and destruction in the Crescent City. Instead, the report concludes that MRGO could not have been responsible for increasing the height of the storm surge by more than a few inches, while subsidence had reduced the height of some of the floodwalls by two feet. Despite being over 7,000 pages long, however, the *Performance Evaluation* devotes remarkably little attention to the role that wetlands once played in protecting New Orleans from hurricane damage.[1]

Another report that took slightly longer to prepare and that came from a different group of experts—the American Society of Civil Engineers (ASCE)—was at least represented by the chair of the study committee as supporting the official views of the Corps. The report itself, which was delivered in June 2007, contained little specific discussion of the effects of MRGO on the destruction of New Orleans, but the chair of the study committee, Dr. David Daniel, president of the University of Texas at Dallas, was less restrained. He attacked the arguments by local residents that the Mississippi River–Gulf Outlet served as a "hurricane highway," characterizing these views as being "commonly held misperceptions" about the Katrina disaster. By contrast, he emphasized the "good news" that he saw as having been inappropriately overlooked. "On the contrary," he stressed, "the modeling indicated that following Katrina, the MRGO enhanced the post-storm drainage of surge waters from flooded New Orleans *back out to the Gulf.*" Still, at least according to press accounts, he seems not to have discussed how MRGO could have been so helpful in letting out the floodwaters while not first having let them in.[2]

Perhaps that is one of the reasons why Dr. Daniel's press release did so little to silence the criticism of MRGO. Another reason, as expressed in a strongly worded editorial response from the *New Orleans Times-Picayune* entitled "Sound bites and spin jobs," may have been the belief that the press release should have represented the actual contents of the report—which in turn could have been more consistent with the models reviewed in the analysis. Several months later, the ASCE report came under scrutiny for another reason. In March 2008, an independent nonprofit group known as Levees.org made public the records they obtained through a request under the Freedom of Information Act. Those records revealed that the U.S. Army Corps of Engineers had paid the group more than $1.1 million for doing their relatively simple review and then publicizing the findings.[3]

Perhaps the key point, though, is that most investigations by independent experts—defined here as those that have come from sources other than the Corps or its contractors—tend to have come to very different conclusions about MRGO.[4]

Although the debates over MRGO have often been technical as well as intense, the underlying issues are reasonably straightforward, and they become visible at the place where MRGO joins the GIWW, or the Gulf Intracoastal Waterway, forming what many locals have come to call "the funnel." The short section to the west of that point is often called the "GIWW Reach," given that this channel, running under the Paris Road Bridge toward the center of New Orleans, combines MRGO and the Gulf Intracoastal Waterway. In the other direction from that same spot, the GIWW heads toward the east-northeast, while the longer stretch of MRGO splits off from the GIWW, heading diagonally to the southeast, down toward the Gulf of Mexico. A map of the two waterways thus does look more than a little like a funnel, lying on its side, with the "bottom" end pointing into the Industrial Canal, directly toward the heart of New Orleans. Perhaps tellingly, while the Corps calls this the "GIWW Reach" of MRGO, locals sometimes call it simply "the hypodermic needle"— the portion of the canal that injects the floodwaters into the main part of the city.

The biggest differences between the Corps and independent observers, though, have to do with the portion of MRGO that heads to the southeast from the throat of the funnel, involving what the Corps calls "MRGO Reach 2." Note especially the references to "Reach 2" in the agency's most comprehensive assessment—but note also the sudden shift to a conclusion regarding the entire "MRGO channel" in the last sentence of the following quotation:

> Three previous studies have been performed to examine the influence of MRGO/*Reach 2* on storm surge in New Orleans and vicinity. . . . All studies have reached the same conclusion. The change in storm surge induced by MRGO/*Reach 2* . . . is greatest when the amplitude

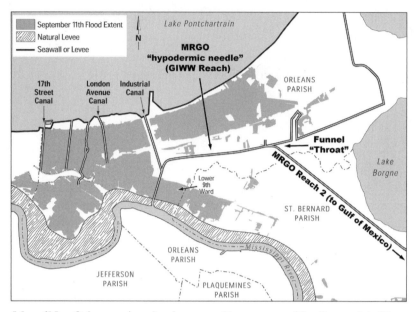

Map of New Orleans region, showing natural levee, extent of flooding, and the "Funnel" and two Reaches of MRGO. Original cartography by Cliff Duplechin. Source: World Watch *Magazine, Vol. 20, No. 5, Sept/Oct 2007, www.worldwatch.org.*

of the storm surge is low, on the order of 4 ft or less. . . . For storm surges of a magnitude produced by Hurricanes Betsy and Katrina, which overwhelmed the wetland system, the influence of MRGO/ *Reach 2* on storm surge propagation is quite small. . . . For large surge-producing storm events, construction of *the MRGO channel* has little influence on water levels in the metropolitan New Orleans vicinity, and in the IHNC [Inner Harbor Navigation (Industrial) Canal] (emphasis added).[5]

A simple translation is that, if the entire marsh is buried under 12–20 feet of water, even the effect of a large channel below the inundation is likely to be modest. That point is a legitimate one, as far as it goes—but as the old saying has it, the devil is in the details.

The Corps report includes two caveats, although the Corps does not call them that. First, as noted in the italicized portions of the quote above, the agency's analyses effectively exclude the GIWW

Reach, or the portion of MRGO that points directly toward the heart of the city. Second, as the Corps notes, its studies have all employed the ADvanced CIRCulation (ADCIRC) model, which is "a two-dimensional, depth-integrated, finite element, hydrodynamic circulation code for ocean shelves, coasts, and estuaries." In simpler English, the long string of technicalities means that the Corps used a model designed for large bodies of water, not for canals or wetlands.[6]

Technically speaking, then, it may well be accurate to say that *this* limited model indicates "little influence" for MRGO in the case of large storms. This model, however, largely ignores the effects of the GIWW reach, and perhaps more importantly, it pays no attention to any damage that MRGO may already have done to what were once healthy wetlands along "Reach 2"—a point to which we will soon return. It also ignores the findings of models that are better suited to wetland regions.

A particularly impressive example is the modeling by Dr. Hassan Mashriqui—a hydrological modeling specialist who was at Louisiana State University's Hurricane Center at the time of Katrina, and who is a native of one of the few other places on the planet where the predominant landforms resemble those of southern Louisiana, namely Bangladesh. Building on extensive experience with flooding in the low-lying coastal regions of his native land, Mashriqui has found that it can be highly misleading to use models that were developed for open oceans, or for that matter for ordinary river flooding, in an effort to predict what can happen when a hurricane hits a low-lying coastal region like New Orleans.

For the GIWW Reach of MRGO, in particular, Mashriqui's modeling has shown that the critical issues include not just the surge *height*, but also the *volume* and *velocity* of water that can come shooting into the heart of the city. Thinking about the difference between the amounts of water that can flow through a soda straw versus a garden hose can offer a useful analogy: even if the Corps is correct in claiming that the water level to the east of the funnel was raised by only a fraction of a foot by "Reach 2" of MRGO, a simple examination of its cross-section shows that well over ten times as much water would have been able to come through the GIWW Reach—which had been expanded to MRGO dimensions—as through the other stretches of the GIWW.*

Far more serious, however, was the damage that MRGO delivered to the region's wetlands.

Salt, Soil, and Spin

In the 1940s, a popular Bourbon Street bar, Pat O'Brien's, created a potent rum-and-fruit-juice concoction called a "hurricane." The bar's official informational materials state that the drink's name was inspired not by the storms, but by the characteristic shape of the glasses in which it is served, which resemble old-fashioned hurricane lamps. Despite that official disclaimer, however, generations of revelers have come to think of the drink as a perfect way to wait out the ferocious tropical storms of the same name.

Part of the reason why both the tourists and the residents could have developed such a relaxed attitude about the name is that, from the time when New Orleans was first settled by Europeans up through at least the time when tourists started to think of a "hurricane" as a drink, New Orleans was protected by two layers of defense—a thin ring of levees and floodwalls, constructed by humans, and a broader band of wetlands, which had been constructed by the Mississippi River over thousands of years. By the time the drink was invented, unfortunately, the outer layer of defenses was starting to show signs

---

*These calculations can quickly get technical, but the basics are quite straightforward. A reasonable estimate is that the cross-sectional area for this Reach of the canal (the "opening size" of the garden hose) was roughly 575 by 36 feet, or an area of 20,700 square feet. By contrast, a canal with the dimensions of the rest of the GIWW—12 feet by 150 feet—would offer a cross-sectional area of 1,800 square feet, or less than one-tenth as large. To come up with final estimates, the relevant experts will eventually need to factor in the loss of the "friction" from the area's wetlands and cypress swamps that were healthy before the construction of MRGO, consider the volumes of water flowing above rather than "in" the canals, and factor in the physical fact that an opening of 20,000 square feet can carry more than ten times as much volume as one of 1,800, because the ratio of "side friction" to flow decreases as the "hose" gets larger. For those who are not interested in such technicalities, the key point is that a much larger canal can deliver far more water, and do so at a much higher speed.

of wear and tear. By the time of Hurricane Betsy, in 1965, the warning signs were starting to become ominous. Of all the physical changes taking place in southeastern Louisiana between 1965 and 2005, finally, probably the most dramatic alterations involved the accelerating losses of the region's wetlands.

Stretching across the southern edge of Louisiana today are vast stretches of former wetlands—once ecologically productive, and protective for the settlements located behind them—that have now turned into open water. Even as recently as the 1950s, Louisiana still had the vast majority of the wetlands that had greeted the French explorers four centuries earlier, but by then the state was losing its land at a rate of 10–15 square miles per year. By the late 1960s, the land was disappearing three to four times faster, with an estimated 45 square miles of coastal wetlands vanishing every year. Louisiana would ultimately lose some 1,700 square miles of wetlands over the last half of the twentieth century—over 1 million of the 5 million acres that were present at the start of the century, or about as much land as had been built up by the Mississippi over the previous 1,000 years.[7]

That is an area nearly as large as Delaware.

In recent years, the land has continued to disappear at the rate of about one U.S. football field every 30 to 45 seconds, 2 to 3 square miles every month, and 30 square miles—more land than Manhattan Island—every year. By the time Katrina hit, the once-thick band of wetlands was in tatters—and after Katrina hit, so was the city of New Orleans.[8]

Climate change was a small part of the reason, and it is likely to become a much bigger part of the story over the years ahead, but climate change was not a major influence over most of the twentieth century. Instead, three other factors played more important roles. One, as already noted, involved humans' alterations to the river's plumbing system—the building of numerous dams and levees along the Mississippi and Missouri rivers—dramatically lowering the amount of sediment reaching southern Louisiana, and keeping the rest contained between the levees, shooting it out into the Gulf of Mexico instead of allowing it to spread across the landscape during flood events. These changes shifted the overall balance between the buildup and loss of land, tilting it for the first time in thousands of years toward loss.

The second had to do with oil exploration and development, which contributed to the loss of coastal wetlands through a proverbial death by a thousand cuts. Early oil drilling was done from platforms that were built on pilings, which in turn were driven into the bottoms of coastal bays and estuaries. That approach, however, was expensive, leading to high and non-recoverable costs of platform construction, even in the case of dry holes. The solution came from a clever invention known as a submersible drilling rig—essentially an ordinary drilling rig that was welded to a barge, which could be towed to the drilling site and sunk. With the top surface of the barge remaining above the surface of the water, and with the aid of a strategically placed slot in the bottom, the drilling could be done from the partially submerged barge. Once the drilling was complete, the barge could be refloated and moved to a new location.

In the four decades between 1937 and 1977, approximately 6,300 exploratory wells and over 21,000 development wells were drilled in the eight Louisiana coastal parishes. Still, these wells could never have been drilled without another invention that appeared in 1938—a barge-mounted dragline—that unfortunately also proved to be highly effective in destroying wetlands. The draglines carved an ever-growing network of canals and pipeline corridors—the "thousand cuts" noted above—that provided ways for the drilling barges to be moved into the marshes and for the oil and gas to be moved out. In many cases, the canals and pipeline corridors allowed salt water to reach and kill salt-intolerant plants in formerly freshwater marshes. In other cases, the dredging created continuous "spoil" piles along the banks of the canals, keeping the marshes from draining normally after heavy rainfalls and thus killing plants that could survive short periods of inundation but not long ones. Overall, although there is no definitive figure on the overall level of damage created by oil-exploration practices, that damage is clearly significant.[9]

Particularly to the southeast of New Orleans, however—the direction from which the most deadly of Katrina's storm surges attacked the city—most non-Corps experts and concerned local citizens have concluded that it was a third type of human intervention that proved most significant. With the possible exception of the kinds of coastal wetland losses that have been predicted but not yet seen in the region from global climate disruption, it would be difficult to imagine another threat to the wetlands that could be more significant than MRGO.

After the St. Bernard Parish Police Jury acted in 1958 to reverse its earlier statement of support for the project, the Corps of Engineers and the local backers of MRGO dismissed the concerns as inconsequential and ill-informed. In the words of a much later, post-Katrina article in the *New Orleans Times-Picayune*, "The parish's fears were dismissed by channel-backers, including The Times-Picayune, which stated in a later editorial that saltwater intrusion into freshwater marshes was 'not to be feared.'" In retrospect, however, it has become clear even a dogged determination to be brave about saltwater intrusion was not enough to keep out the actual salt—and certainly not enough to keep the salt from killing the plants that formerly helped to keep the fragile soils in place.[10]

The initial excavation of MRGO required the moving of more than 270 million cubic yards of dirt—more dirt than was moved in constructing the Panama Canal. That initial excavation, unfortunately, proved to be only the start of an ever-expanding spiral of losses.

Part of the problem appears to have been that the new navigation canal was designed, in the words of Azcona, to be nearly as "straight as an engineer's ruler." The net effect of this design feature was that, ironically, the supposed "outlet" of MRGO actually became instead a truly major "inlet." As a "slackwater" ditch—one that had no flow to keep out salt water—MRGO became the perfect shortcut for saltwater intrusion.[11]

Once the initial opening of the canal reached salt water, MRGO began to provide regular deliveries of salt with each high tide, with extra doses being brought in during major storms. That fact, in turn, created deadly ecological consequences. A particularly important loss involved the region's once-plentiful cypress trees, which can live for 700 years under "normal" conditions, and which are utterly unfazed by freshwater inundation, but which can easily be killed by salt water. Within a few years from the time when MRGO was officially declared to be complete, a noted wetlands expert, Sherwood Gagliano, would be reporting to officials of St. Bernard Parish—and presenting the key findings at a large public meeting regarding a proposal for the Corps to deepen the channel—that the construction of MRGO had already caused a "funnel" effect that could worsen the effects of storm surges, and that it had already contributed to dramatic increases in salinity. By 1999, an assessment by the Corps of Engineers itself found that MRGO had brought brackish conditions—intermediate levels of salinity, which cypress trees could no longer survive—to more than 11,000 acres of marshes and cypress swamps that formerly had low levels of salinity. In addition, more than 19,000 acres of previously brackish marshes were turned into saline ones—a fact that spelled a similar salty death for many of the kinds of plants that can ordinarily survive in brackish marshes.[12]

The changes started even before MRGO was officially declared complete. At Shell Beach, near the middle of the canal, salinity levels leaped upward, rising from an average of 3.5 parts per thousand (PPT) in 1959–1961 to an average of 12 PPT in 1962–1964. What may be more important than the specific numbers, or the fact that salinity levels more than tripled, is that the new levels of salinity were more than sufficient to kill the region's cypress trees.[13]

Just as critics had forecast, moreover, once the plants died, their roots no longer held together the fragile marsh soils, which is one of the reasons why the dredging of MRGO has been such an ongoing challenge. The massive quantities of the fragile wetland soils removed by the Corps during the original excavation of MRGO proved to be not so much the "completion" of the process, but the beginning.

The land losses mounted so rapidly that even the official designation of 1968 as the "completion" date for MRGO is essentially arbitrary. Roughly as fast as the channel would be "finished," more mud and silt would slide into the channel, requiring it to be dredged again, and again, just to maintain the shipping channel at its designed depth—an annual expense that, as previously noted, was not accurately reflected in the project's original benefit-cost assessment, but also one that served to make the initial problems even worse.

The problem was related to the fact that MRGO's original engineers used unrealistic estimates of the ability of the wetland soils to support steep canal walls. Their official design called for MRGO to have a surface width of 625 feet, on the theory that this would somehow allow the Corps to maintain a 36-foot-deep channel that would be 500 feet wide at its bottom. That would have been an impossibly optimistic miscalculation for such soft soil under any circumstances, but it was a particularly flawed estimate for an area where saltwater intrusion would be poisoning ever-broadening expanses of what had once been soil-holding plants—and for a canal that, after all, was supposed to serve large ships. In cases where ships did use the channel, the long stretches of the soft mud along the banks of the canal were pounded by waves from the wakes of passing vessels, making the problem still worse. The *Louisiana: Ecosystem Restoration Study*— issued by the Corps itself in late 2004, just a few months before Katrina—calculated that the ship traffic caused the north bank of the canal to erode at a rate of 35 feet per year, leading to "the direct loss of approximately 100 acres of shoreline brackish marsh every year and additional losses of interior wetlands and shallow ponds."[14]

What emerged, in sum, was a vicious and self-reinforcing cycle. As salt water killed off the plants that had formerly helped to hold together the fragile soils, the surrounding wetlands would continue to slump into the channel—requiring yet another year of dredging by the Corps, after which the channel surface would grow even wider. After that, still more salt water would surge into the marshes, destroying still more plant life. As the soils disappeared from the surrounding marshland and into the channel, MRGO continued to widen, spreading as fast as a typical American's waistline. By the time Katrina hit, much of the channel—including the area closest to New Orleans—would be nearly half a mile across.

As the plants and then the soil disappeared, so did much of the original wildlife. As noted by Caffey and LeBlanc, "pre-project inventories depict fresh and intermediate marshes as once supporting more than two hundred and fifty thousand over-wintering ducks and an annual fur harvest of more than six hundred fifty thousand animals." Later inventories began to show declines even before MRGO was completed. By 1965, the regional shrimp fishery had shifted from predominantly white shrimp to more salt-tolerant brown shrimp, probably because the nursery grounds for the shrimp, in the estuaries, had

Aerial view of GIWW (narrower channel, running left-right) and MRGO "funnel," looking toward the south, as taken in the fall of 2007. The dotted line indicates the approximate initial width of MRGO channel, which along this stretch had eroded to become more than half a mile wide by the time of Hurricane Katrina. Photograph by Robert Gramling.

become increasingly saline. By 1968, the year when the Corps finally pronounced the construction complete, ten species of fish with low tolerance for salinity had already disappeared from routine sampling. Oyster production moved inland—where the oysters (and hence the humans eating those oysters) became increasingly susceptible to bacterial contamination. Other species suffered as well—and by the time of Katrina, it would become clear that humans were among the species being harmed.[15]

Some sense of the habitat losses can be gained from a series of historic aerial photographs of the area just to the south of the "hypodermic needle," made available by researchers from the University of Wisconsin. Of particular note is the area that the Wisconsin researchers call the Bayou Bienvenue triangle, which lies just to the southwest of the MRGO funnel, meaning that it also lies immediately to the north of the developed areas of the Lower Ninth Ward and adjacent St. Bernard Parish.

In the earliest available photograph, from 1933, there was little evidence of development even along the Industrial Canal (which is visible along the left side of this and the following photographs). By 1952, the Gulf Intracoastal Waterway had been connected to the Industrial Canal, which was beginning to be the home to significantly more development, but the picture otherwise looked quite similar. As of 1960—by which time the Mississippi River was sufficiently well-contained within levees that the area was no longer receiving new deposits of silt, construction had begun on MRGO, and oil and gas development would have been well under way—the last available aerial photograph from before the completion of MRGO showed a much wider GIWW reach, along with what appears to have been a degree of degradation in what had been unbroken cypress swamps just a few years later. The largest change in the Bayou Bienvenue triangle, however, would take place between 1960 and 1976—the time of the next available photograph in the sequence—by which time this patch of wetlands would see more change than it had in all recorded history up to that time. Like so many other wetland areas in the vicinity of MRGO, this one had by that time turned into open water.

As discussed in Chapter 5, the saga of MRGO went on for many decades. During that time, backers held numerous public meetings, presentations, dinner parties, and other events to build support for the canal. Those events, however, seem to have been a bit selective in their openness to local input: they took place mainly in New Orleans or in Washington, DC. Tellingly, none seems to have taken place in St. Bernard Parish—even though, as noted earlier, this parish was the jurisdiction that was slated to be the actual location for MRGO. Initially, this pattern might simply have reflected the fact that Growth Machine elites in New Orleans considered the parish residents to be unimportant. As local concern grew, however, particularly after Hurricane Betsy, St. Bernard Parish became a place where MRGO boosters would have had an increasingly hard time finding much support.[16]

The contrast between the views of the channel's backers and the

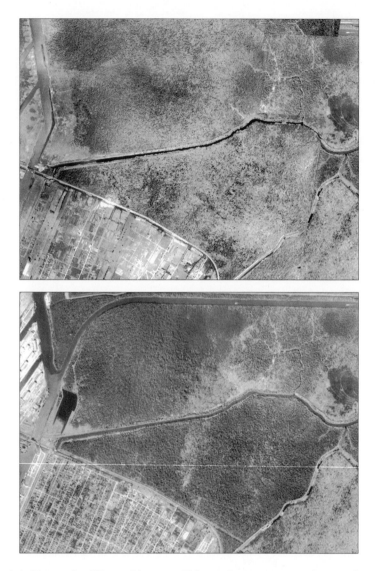

Aerial photographs of "Bayou Bienvenue Triangle," taken 1933, 1952 (this page), 1960, and 1976 (next page). In the earliest photograph, from 1933, there is little development even along the Industrial Canal (at the far left). By 1952, the Gulf Intracoastal Waterway had been connected to the Industrial Canal, which was beginning to see significantly more development. As of 1960—by which time construction had begun on MRGO, the development of oil and gas facilities in the region was well under way, and the river was sufficiently well contained within levees that it was no longer able to deposit new silt in the area—the last available aerial photograph from before the

completion of MRGO shows some degradation in what had been unbroken cypress swamps just a few years earlier. By 1976, however, the first photograph available after the construction of MRGO showed that the marsh had clearly changed more than it had in all recorded history up to that time, having largely turned into open water. All photographs courtesy of Louisiana State University Cartographic Information Center; New Orleans Public Library; TerraServer-USA, Microsoft Corp., and U.S. Geological Survey, as compiled by Natalie Hunt and Travis Scott, working under the direction of Dr. Herbert Wang, University of Wisconsin.

Corps of Engineers, on the one hand, and of independent analysts and residents of the directly affected region, on the other, may actually provide an example of a broader pattern. As is the case with any number of other so-called economic development projects, whatever incentives the projects' backers may have for disregarding any bad news, such incentives may not apply to the ordinary citizens who live in the affected region—the ones who are the most likely to see and experience the damage firsthand.

That does in fact appear to be what happened in St. Bernard Parish. Edwin Roy's crusading editorials in the *Voice* showed considerable foresight, and the flooding from Hurricane Betsy provided initial evidence that his concerns should have been taken seriously. Early scientific studies, such as environmental report prepared for the parish by Sherwood Gagliano in 1972 appears to have identified the environmental problems of MRGO with impressive clarity. Still, as the actual environmental damage from MRGO began to spread, even ordinary eyesight was enough to permit increasing numbers of the parish's residents to see the evidence that the channel's backers were unwilling or unable to see.[17]

Only three main roads connected low-lying St. Bernard Parish to the outside world, and one of them, which connects the parish to Interstate 10, crosses over the GIWW Reach on what locals call the Paris Road Bridge. Given that this bridge is high enough to permit ships to pass below, it has also offered a clear view of the progressive loss of once-healthy wetlands. Local residents could also see what was happening when they visited the seafood restaurants and other businesses along the same road, just to the south of the high-rise bridge. Thanks to the growing influence of MRGO, more open water was created, and after several years, the waves started lapping against the roadway even during minor storms. In response, authorities raised the road's surface, and ordinary residents started to worry even more about MRGO's effects.

As MRGO's environmental damage became too vivid for the people of St. Bernard Parish to ignore, the lack of enthusiasm for MRGO also became increasingly clear. By 1998, underscoring its earlier opposition, the St. Bernard Parish Council unanimously called for the channel's closing. Half a dozen years later, in May of 2004,

Southeastern Louisiana University conducted a poll of St. Bernard voters, asking them to identify "the most important problem facing the people of St. Bernard Parish today." Even though the poll was taken more than a year before Katrina would strike, MRGO was one of the three problems mentioned most often, with only illegal drugs and the lack of jobs being more worrisome.[18]

In the broader region as well, the apparently widespread support that greeted the initial announcements of the project started to disappear along with the wetlands. The earliest investigation and meetings by the St. Bernard Police Jury in 1957–1958, and the expressions of concern at the U.S. Department of Interior during the same years, would be the first of literally hundreds of studies, warnings, and meetings. By the 1990s, even the *Times-Picayune*—once an enthusiastic booster of Growth Machine proposals, but eventually a much more balanced newspaper—hired a number of widely respected journalists, including Mark Schleifstein and John McQuaid, whose stories on the growing environmental problems of the region would win Pulitzer Prizes and prestigious awards from the American Society of Civil Engineers, the American Association for the Advancement of Science, and the American Institute of Biological Sciences.

As part of its expanded and more evenhanded approach, the paper devoted extensive coverage to a series of community meetings that were becoming increasingly commonplace during the fifteen years before Katrina would hit. One story, for example, took note of "Property Owners Fed Up With Land-Eating Channel": "Since the MRGO was dug in the 1960s as a shortcut for Gulf of Mexico shipping, Donald DeBouchel has watched the channel eat away 30 acres of St. Bernard Parish cypress swamp his grandfather bought in 1878."[19]

Another *Times-Picayune* story covered a meeting where the president of the Port of New Orleans—an organization rarely noted in previous years for its "good neighbor" policies toward St. Bernard Parish—offered "Pledges to Help Fight MRGO Erosion":

> Sportsmen, conservationists, commercial fishermen and residents banded together Thursday to speak out against environmental problems they say have been created by the MRGO. About 300 people attended the meeting in Chalmette organized by the St. Bernard Sportsmen's League and the Lake Pontchartrain Basin Foundation.

A healthy cypress swamp. Note that these trees are growing and thriving even in standing (but fresh) water. It is easy to see why experts estimate that a band of healthy cypress trees one mile wide could reduce a storm's surge by roughly a foot. Photograph by Robert Gramling/All Rights Reserved.

As an interim step, Port President Gary LaGrange announced an agreement last week with St. Bernard Parish President Henry "Junior" Rodriguez to build a massive gate across the MRGO and keep it dredged to 28 feet. Many St. Bernard residents voiced opposition to the agreement, and the Parish Council on Thursday rejected it, instead calling for the MRGO to be filled in entirely.[20]

Today, it is difficult to miss the evidence that environmentalists and critics of MRGO were far more accurate in their expectations than were the canal's backers. The net results of MRGO include eerie sights of death and destruction in the former cypress swamps, with the disappearing remains of cypress groves offering an unsettling parallel to, as well as a cause of, the death and destruction that poured into New Orleans. Thousands of acres of formerly healthy cypress trees have become home instead to what many locals call "ghost swamps," filled not by strong and healthy trees, but by a few scattered skeletons of once-healthy ones.

Dead remnants of trees that no longer protect St. Bernard Parish and Lower Ninth Ward, as seen from 40-Arpent Levee. Photograph by William Freudenburg/All Rights Reserved.

Based on estimates from the Corps that were summarized above, a report by the Congressional Research Service has concluded that MRGO has destroyed nearly 23,000 acres of Louisiana's coastal wetlands, while significantly raising salinity levels in over 30,000 acres more—a total footprint of more than 50,000 acres. Other estimates have concluded MRGO was single-handedly responsible for the destruction or severe degradation of roughly 65,000 acres of wetlands—an area that would represent just over 100 square miles out of the 500 square miles of wetlands that had provided New Orleans with a vital triangle of shelter and shock-absorption before the Corps began construction of MRGO.[21]

Making matters worse, the lion's share of this destruction took place in the very quadrant of the compass from which the damage to New Orleans from Hurricane Katrina would be the most severe, namely the southeast. Without the loss of miles of marshes and cypress swamps, the storm surge that hit the city might have been several feet lower, and New Orleans might still be largely intact today. In a very real sense, MRGO proved to be the single cut that led to a thousand deaths.

The Problem and the Prediction

On May 19, 2005—about two weeks before the official June 1 start of the 2005 hurricane season, or three months before Katrina hit— Hassan Mashriqui from LSU's Hurricane Center made a presentation at the Eastbank Public Library in Jefferson Parish, just to the west of New Orleans. The meeting had been called by the Southeast Louisiana Regional Planning Commission, an organization led by the presidents of the five metropolitan-area parishes. Most such meetings are notable mainly for the levels of technical detail they contain and for the levels of boredom they inspire, but in this case, the session had been called to discuss "Hurricane Vulnerability Modeling for Southeast Louisiana." Although attendance was by invitation only, and publicity had been minimal, the room was full.

At that meeting, in the clearest terms he knew how to muster, Dr. Mashriqui warned that metropolitan New Orleans faced truly serious risks. He focused on the "funnel effect," just to the east of the city, where his calculations had led him to conclude that a hurricane's storm surges, rather than being just a few inches higher than elsewhere, could be amplified by as much as 20–40 percent.

It is easy to understand that the Corps of Engineers might not have been eager to hear such a message. The funnel effect had been created in part by additional hurricane-protection levees that the Corps had begun to build around New Orleans soon after Hurricane Betsy in 1965. With encouragement from local Growth Machine and real-estate-development interests, the Corps had agreed at that time to build hurricane-protection levees along the north bank of the GIWW, providing apparent protection for the portion of Orleans Parish known by locals as "New Orleans East," although it was largely uninhabited at the time: "Such an enclosure would let developers reclaim land and give the city growing room. A later study found that only 21 percent of the land the Corps's new system would enclose

"Ghost swamps," no longer protecting downtown New Orleans, as seen from Bayou Bienvenue. Photograph © Bevil Knapp/All Rights Reserved.

was already inhabited. Millions of dollars would be spent protecting empty space."[22]

By the time those decisions were made, however, MRGO was in its last stages of construction, and engineering projections had already shown that protection of St. Bernard Parish and the Lower Ninth Ward would require a levee along the southwestern flank of MRGO. The net effect of these two levees was to produce the funnel effect noted above, meaning that an ironic if presumably unintended effect of the Corps's "hurricane protection" system was to worsen some of the potential risks of hurricane-related flooding.

As noted in the opening pages of this book, most of the actual death and destruction from a hurricane is due to water, particularly its "storm surge," which is not a wave like a tidal wave, but more like a bulge, or an extremely high tide. This bulge was what Katrina's winds shoved into the constriction in the funnel—and it was what then surged through the GIWW Reach and into the Industrial Canal as the eye of Katrina roared past. At that point, the water appears to have done what it usually does when too much water gets poured into a funnel, too fast—it went spilling over the top, as well as shooting into and over the Industrial Canal, where it became a sudden threat to survival in the Lower Ninth Ward.

Some of the storm water also ripped through the MRGO levee itself, particularly near the throat of the funnel. A particularly telling example involves a floodgate across the same Bayou Bienvenue featured in the historic photographs of the Bayou Bienvenue triangle. In the immediate aftermath of Katrina, and for a surprisingly long time thereafter, the official position of the Corps was that the large breach at this spot was opened "deliberately" (although by persons the Corps never named), to help the marsh to drain. A complicating factor for that line of argument, on the other hand, is that aerial photographs taken by the National Oceanic and Atmospheric Administration (NOAA) less than a week after Katrina's landfall, show that there would be no need to dig a breach at that location—given the existence of floodgates that could simply be opened—but also that the "deliberate" breach had included the remarkably extensive removal of virtually every speck of dirt that had previously been piled up on both sides of the concrete wall that remained. The position of the Corps is still harder to accept in light of the fact that the kinds of heavy equipment that would have been required to remove so much soil, so fast, were badly needed, but notable mainly by their absence at the time—something that continued to be true for months after Katrina, let alone the first week. Later, in a public briefing for citizens of the New Orleans region, the Corps itself included a photo of the same breach, complete with the barge that was left stranded on the top of the levee—and complete as well with a date stamp showing that it had been taken on September 1, just three days after Katrina.

The more plausible interpretation is again provided by Mashriqui and his colleagues from the LSU Hurricane Center, whose modeling indicated that the highest velocities through the hurricane-protection levee were those that occurred on the southwestern side of the "funnel throat," where "the wingwall . . . failed and resulted in scour 50 feet deep."[23] Although the exact water levels of Katrina's surge in the Industrial Canal and the confluence of the funnel can only be estimated, Masrhiqui's calculations, as spelled out in subsequent interviews, indicate that the funnel effect did significantly

September 1, 2005, photo of Bayou Bienvenue breach, looking along MRGO Levee, toward the southeast, as used in Corps presentation to New Orleans residents. Photograph courtesy of U.S. Army Corps of Engineers, New Orleans District.

increase elevations and velocities, just as citizen critics have charged all along.[24]

While the Corps has consistently disputed the criticisms of MRGO, the agency did make one important change in its stance as the third hurricane season after Katrina was approaching. That was when, in a sudden move that surprised many, the Corps tentatively approved an ambitious plan, expected to cost $695 million, to keep water away from the throat of the funnel by building a huge concrete wall across the damaged wetlands east of the GIWW Reach. The construction of that barrier was well under way by the time this book went to press.[25]

When he was making his presentation to the Regional Planning Commission, Dr. Mashriqui joined other hazard researchers over the years who have taken on roles as citizen scientists seeking to contribute to public safety. He had repeatedly been rebuffed in his past attempts but hoped that, since he had been invited to present his work to the commission, his warning might be heard more clearly this time around. As he subsequently described the results of that evening's presentation to a reporter from the *Washington Post*, "I told everyone: if New Orleans is a boat, here are the holes. . . . This is my passion; I don't want people to die in hurricanes. But nobody did anything."

As the article in the *Post* went on to note, it was not strictly true that no one did *anything*: Corps officials did respond, but they did so by telling him they were not permitted to study anything that was not within their congressional authorization. One colleague of Mashirqui's at the LSU Hurricane Center also did something. He predicted that nothing would happen until hundreds of people died.[26]

Beginning just 102 days later, some fifteen hundred people did just that.

Chapter 8

Critical for
Economic Survival?

Iɴ Kᴀᴛʀɪɴᴀ's immediate aftermath, the media carried many reports of "looting problems." In retrospect, it became clear that much of the looting involved food, water, medical supplies, and other necessities, which—given that the stores were closed and flooded—were simply not otherwise available to the stranded survivors. It is also clear that some of the looting did involve expensive luxuries, such as plasma-screen televisions, with no such survival benefits—although it is not clear how much benefit the looters could have derived from such contraband in a city with no electricity, and in which some areas would still not see the restoration of electric service for years. With the benefit of hindsight, however, perhaps the clearest conclusion that can be drawn is that the most serious looting of all was done not by poor blacks, but by rich whites—both in terms of contributing to the risks, in advance of Katrina, and in terms of taking advantage of the recovery afterward.

To date, relatively greater attention has been devoted to the latter pattern, which might well be called "aftermath looting." One example, which was first revealed by the *New Orleans Times-Picayune*, involved FEMA's "Operation Blue Roof," which paid contractors to patch damaged roofs by nailing on temporary plastic tarps that were usually blue. At least three of FEMA's prime contractors got payments that ranged between $149 and $175 per "square" (an area of ten feet by ten feet). Locally, these rates are comparable to the costs for completely new roofs, not to what would ordinarily be paid for pounding a few nails through temporary tarps—but that was only the beginning of "the magic of the marketplace." Each of these contractors then subcontracted the jobs to other companies—generally after having kept about half of the cash as compensation for their trouble. Those "round one" subcontractors then further subcontracted to other firms, after keeping about half of what they were being paid, and so on. Finally, the firms at the very bottom of the feeding-frenzy chain— those who did the actual work—earned as little as $2 per square, or about what such a temporary patching job would ordinarily be expected to cost.[1]

A similar pattern was documented for debris removal. A company with well-connected lobbyists obtained a $500 million contract for debris removal—an amount that calculates to about $23 per cubic yard. That company in turn hired another, to which it paid $9 per cubic yard—and subsequent layers of subcontractors were then paid $8, $7, and ultimately just $3 per cubic yard. Most of what got "hauled," in short, was taxpayer money, not debris.[2]

Not even the dead were spared the indignity of such "efficiencies." Soon after photos of victims' bodies started to create public-relations headaches, a no-bid contract was awarded to Kenyon International Emergency Services—a wholly owned subsidiary of a funeral-services firm in Texas headed by Robert Waltrip, a close friend of the Bush family. Over a period of two months, Kenyon recovered 535 bodies, or about a third of the total number of the known Katrina casualties in Louisiana. The company "billed the state of Louisiana over $6 million for its services, or about $12,500 per victim . . . [but] dozens of bodies that Kenyon missed continue to be found by local authorities and in some cases, family members. Meanwhile, local black morticians volunteered their services to help in recovery and processing of bodies, but were turned away by Federal Emergency Management Agency (FEMA)." Only after the federal funds ran out were the local black morticians taken up on their generous offer, which they fulfilled by transporting the final unidentified victims to the mausoleum of the Katrina memorial on Canal Boulevard.[3]

In terms of actual dollar amounts, however, the greater looting was done by the Growth Machine proponents who had worked so hard, for so many years, to bring in hundreds of millions of federal dollars for building and maintaining MRGO. Like the earliest looters of New Orleans, around the time of Jean Lafitte, these boosters obtained most of their loot from people who lived outside of the region, although Lafitte procured most of his plunder from Spanish shipping interests, while the boosters took their treasure from fellow American taxpayers. Like many of the survivors who "looted" medical supplies and food, few of the boosters saw themselves as doing something morally wrong, while—unlike the looters or for that matter Lafitte—they almost always acted in ways that were legal as well as being widely respected by their fellow citizens. Whatever their levels of respectability and good intentions, unfortunately, their canal-building efforts were not so much a response to the devastation of Katrina as they were one major cause of it.

One reason why their efforts enjoyed so much support—at least in New Orleans, if not so often in St. Bernard Parish—was the commonly held belief that MRGO would contribute mightily to the region's economic vitality. Unlike the environmental concerns that were raised by the channel's opponents, though, the promises of economic benefits from the canal seem to have been accepted with little question—a pattern that, once again, is scarcely limited to New Orleans.[4]

Based on the what can be derived from reading the newspapers of the 1950s and 1960s, there seems to be little evidence that any significant group of people in this case—not even MRGO's most fervent opponents in St. Bernard Parish or in the Louisiana conservation community—seriously questioned the widespread assumption that building more canals would mean building more prosperity. For example, even the "Statement of Concern" about MRGO from the Louisiana Wildlife and Fisheries Commission explicitly accepted the assumption that "the development of this channel will be a beneficial development to navigation," citing as evidence the U.S. Army Corps of Engineers' benefit-cost analysis and a hearing in the U.S. House of Representatives. Unfortunately, although opponents' concerns about the channel's environmental risks turned out to be largely on-target, proponents' promises of economic benefits were not.[5]

Even in the wake of Katrina, at least some politicians did continue to argue for "investing" still more tax money into dredging and "reopening" MRGO, in the name of economic necessity, and local observers interviewed by the *New Orleans Times-Picayune* continued to express the conviction that MRGO would be "unlikely to close." At least among supporters, the usual complaint was not that MRGO was dangerous, but that there simply had not been enough money to build all of the flood-protection projects that the region needed.[6]

That complaint, however, is a bit hard to accept. Between 2000 and 2005, Louisiana actually received far more money for Corps civil works projects than any other state—about $1.9 billion in all, well ahead of the $1.4 billion in second-place California, which has a coastline about three times as long and a population more than seven times as large. A bigger part of the problem is that, instead of hurricane protection, the political system consistently "invested" taxpayers' money in projects that regional politicians saw as offering more immediate payoffs to the broader economy. Former Louisiana Senator John Breaux, for example, told the *Washington Post* that "We thought all the projects were important—not just levees." Although he said that "hindsight" might have pointed to different priorities, "navigation projects were critical to our economic survival."[7]

The Senator may well have believed that claim—and so may some of the social scientists whose first inclination is to characterize projects such as MRGO as serving the interest of "economic growth" or "capitalism," writ large. Whatever benefits the projects may have brought to the region's major political actors and/or their donors, however, the projects' true importance for the "economic survival" of the state proved to be remarkably small. MRGO's actual "contributions" to the economy were more or less in line with the "benefits" once delivered by Lafitte and his fellow pirates—bringing riches to the few, modest advantages to a broader set of beneficiaries, and significantly greater costs than benefits to the economy as a whole.[8]

Making matters worse, evidence about the emptiness of MRGO's economic promise was actually available early enough that much of the channel's damage could have been avoided, if only that evidence had been heeded at the time. It was just two years after the start of construction, for example—eight years before the project's official completion—when the Corps began to notice a problem: the Industrial Canal lock, which formed the Mississippi River connection to MRGO, seemed likely to become obsolete at just about the time that the construction would finally be completed:

> The River and Harbor Act of 1956 authorized the Mississippi River–Gulf Outlet. . . . The 1956 Act also provided for the construction of a new lock and connecting channel when economically justified by obsolescence of the existing lock or by increased traffic. *Studies were initiated in 1960 for a new lock and connecting channel because at that time it was estimated that the lock would become dimensionally obsolete by 1970* (emphasis added).[9]

As suggested earlier, the lock and thus the Industrial Canal and MRGO did indeed soon become "dimensionally obsolete." The key virtue of waterborne transportation is not speed, but the capacity to carry weight and bulk. Both the Industrial Canal and MRGO were planned, initiated, and completed in the midst of a trend in water transportation that probably started when our earliest ancestors first climbed onto a log to ford a river. That trend has continued with ancient European and Asian mariners, the European colonization of the rest of the world, the growth of industrial technology, the early days of steel ships, the massive tankers and container ships that ply the seas today, and ultimately, the even larger ones that are likely to cross those same seas tomorrow. Consistently enough that one might imagine that the overall pattern would seem predictable by now, the trend has reliably involved the tendency of vessels to get bigger, and then bigger again.

According to estimates from the Corps of Engineers, the largest ships that can use the Industrial Canal lock are dry-bulk carriers of less than 20,000 "deadweight tonnage" (dwt), or general-cargo carriers of less than 18,000 dwt (96 percent of ships using the locks are general cargo carriers).* Since 1968, when the Industrial Canal lock began to provide the official access point between MRGO and the Missis-

---

*DWT stands for "deadweight tons." Deadweight, for those who seldom consult shipping industry statistics for leisure reading, is calculated in terms of the displacement of water when a ship is loaded, minus the weight of the ship when empty. Deadweight tonnage, accordingly, includes the ship's crew, passengers, cargo, fuel, water, and stores.

sippi River, the U.S. has seen the construction of just 43 ships having a size of less than 18,000 dwt, as opposed to 258 that have been larger. Of those 43 smaller ships—the only ones small enough to use the lock—just 7 have been constructed since 1981. Perhaps it is not so surprising, then, that only a few businesses remain in operation along the Industrial Canal today.[10]

In the words of the well-known geographer Peirce Lewis, "The Port of New Orleans was plainly falling behind. Facilities that had been heralded as waves of the future in the 1960s and 1970s were now seriously out of date—especially the city's main container port along . . . the Inner Harbor Navigation Canal." In fact, Lewis may have been generous about the "heralding." It actually occurred even before MRGO was finished.[11]

The problem is not simply that the Industrial Canal lock is too small to serve today's oceangoing vessels. The bigger problem is that MRGO itself, with its 36-foot depth limitation, has also been obsolete for decades. For many years, one key constraint on ship size has been imposed by "Panamax" dimensions, involving the 39-foot draft that is the greatest depth permitted by the Panama Canal. That canal, to note the obvious, saves spectacularly more mileage than MRGO. In 2007, however, the nation of Panama began construction on new, larger locks, built to serve ships having up to 50-foot drafts.[12]

In fact, many of the container ships sailing today already require almost 50-foot depths, and larger ones still are on the drawing boards, raising the specter that even the Mississippi River itself—with a draft limit of 45 feet through its opening to the Gulf of Mexico, Southwest Pass—may become increasingly obsolete as well. As Lewis has noted, when the newly appointed head of the Dock Board stepped up to the problem early in the twenty-first century, he proposed that "The best thing to do was to forget about the Inner Harbor container facilities, and to forget about MRGO as well." Subsequent energy and construction has in fact gone into new container facilities on the Mississippi River, where prospects for the future are not as bleak.[13]

For all of its environmental damage and economic cost, meanwhile, MRGO is basically just a very long ditch that runs parallel to the much deeper Mississippi River—and even before MRGO was completed, that river was being dredged continuously, 24 hours a day,

365 days a year, at taxpayer expense. At least the river, however, sees truly significant shipping traffic. The traffic on MRGO, by contrast, started out below the original expectations, and despite increasingly brave claims by MRGO backers that traffic would soon begin to rise, the actual volumes stayed on the low side. Then, after a few years of modest increases, volumes started to drop, and the news was getting even worse during the last few years before Katrina struck. By 2004, the last full year before Katrina, the "economically vital" MRGO carried a mere 1.2 million tons of shipping—just 0.4 percent as much as the Mississippi River. Put another way, although the Mississippi River had been depicted by MRGO proponents, over decades of advocacy, as being almost completely unsuited for shipping, the "fog-covered, silt-bearing, temperamental" river carried more than 250 times as much freight.[14]

Even if we ignore the hundreds of millions of dollars that taxpayers "invested" in MRGO in earlier years, focusing only on the ongoing expenditures for maintenance dredging, the cost of that dredging during fiscal year 2004, alone, came to $19.1 million. According to the Corps' own statistics, meanwhile, *total* traffic on MRGO in 2004, by ships that drew enough water to need the dredging, amounted to fewer than a dozen round trips. Thus that year's cost of dredging alone came to over $1.5 million per round trip—and that would have been before considering the human and environmental costs of the project.[15]

Lafitte would have been amazed.

All Wet?

Although the Corps proposed to start dredging MRGO again after Katrina, Congress ordered instead that the Corps undertake a "de-authorization" study. In its resulting report—the economic analysis for which actually came from its Galveston office, rather than its New Orleans office—the Corps provided the kinds of analyses that had not been seen since the 1930s. The report concluded that neither maintaining "the authorized dimensions of the MRGO," nor maintaining shallower-draft navigation dimensions of the Gulf Intracoastal Waterway (12 feet by 125 feet), would be worth the cost—or

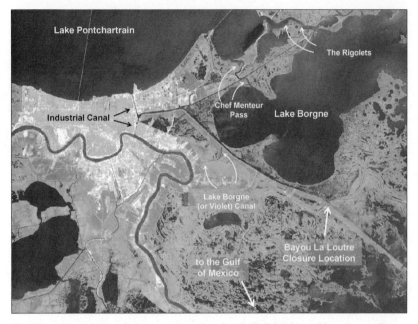

Satellite photo of New Orleans region, showing MRGO "closure" location on Bayou La Loutre Ridge (lower right).

in the standard economic lingo, would be "cost-effective"—due to "irregular use of the MRGO" even by shallow-draft traffic. Given the evidence summarized above, it is hard to avoid the question of how long both of those conclusions had actually been true. Still, even though the conclusions came too late to help the people who lost their homes or their lives in the New Orleans region, the draft final report did finally start to foretell the beginning of the end of MRGO.[16]

What the report did not foretell was an actual "closing" or filling in of MRGO, in the ways that the earlier Carondolet and New Basin canals had been filled in. The reason is that, according to the "very rough estimate" from the Corps, it would take approximately 250–350 million cubic yards of dredged material just to "fill the channel from mile 60 to mile 25." The rough estimate was not just that such a project would cost about $2.8 billion, but also that, "depending on how many scow barges could be used . . . it could take from 15 to 44 years to fill the channel."[17]

Reconstructed Industrial Canal floodwall adjoining the Lower Ninth Ward. Note differences in heights between the newer section of the wall, to the left, versus the "old" or original section/height on the right. Photograph by William Freudenburg.

The implications of the Corps report were not terribly popular in the region, but they were quite straightforward. Even if maintenance dredging is stopped, with MRGO being sealed at the natural levee known as Bayou La Loutre Ridge—a change that had begun by the time this book went to press—both MRGO and its associated eco-logical damage will remain as open wounds in the wetlands, and the threat to New Orleans will continue. The Corps report is straightfor-ward on this point, citing a 2006 study by the Louisiana Department of Natural Resources in the process of noting that merely sealing off one spot along MRGO "would not provide significant, direct mitiga-tion of severe hurricane storm surge."[18]

Other Corps decisions following Katrina have also played badly in the New Orleans region. The GIWW Reach of MRGO, for example—the "hypodermic needle" extending westward from the funnel—was specifically authorized by the Corps to remain at its much larger, MRGO-sized dimensions. In addition, although the Corps upgraded the portions of the floodwall along the Industrial Canal *in the specific locations where they failed*, the remaining floodwalls are at the same height as the sections that failed to hold Katrina's floodwaters.[19]

The draft final report also went back to the long-dormant proposal to enlarge the current Industrial Canal lock—the one that was authorized, but never funded, even though this was the project that led to the declaration from the acting director of the Bureau of the Budget, Elmer Statts, more than half a century ago, that the benefits of the project would be high enough to justify the costs. As the de-authorization report noted, this lock is still authorized. Enlarging that lock would permit the few larger ships still using MRGO to reach the Industrial Canal from the Mississippi River, but it would do so at a taxpayer cost that, by 2007, was estimated to have grown to $764 million. As this book was going to press in 2009, that project was still on hold—with no additional funds having been directed toward it, even in the gigantic economic stimulus bill of early 2009—while a supplemental environmental impact assessment was being prepared.[20]

In fairness, there is a solid practical argument for a new lock on the Industrial Canal, for serving east/west traffic on the GIWW. The Industrial Canal Lock is a significant bottleneck, being well over 80 years old and "dimensionally obsolete." Barge captains often encounter 12- to 14-hour delays in making their way through the lock. Because MRGO serves as the only feasible way for barge traffic to bypass the Industrial Canal Lock when the lock is closed, and because the GIWW is a busy waterway, inland water transportation interests are reluctant to see MRGO closed until a new lock is constructed.[21]

Neighborhoods in the vicinity of the lock, on the other hand, have opposed the idea of building a new lock at the current location ever since the original plans were announced in the 1970s—and the opposition has only intensified in the wake of Hurricane Katrina. Aside from the disruption that can be created by such a massive construction project, residents fear the kinds of contamination that might result from disturbing the bottom sediments that have accumulated over the 80-year life of the Industrial Canal. What they suggest instead is that, if a new lock is to be built, it should be built on the little-used Lake Borgne (Violet) Canal.

What will finally happen in this latest act of the ongoing drama of

Katrina, and what the Corps expects if and when the project is completed, can only be guessed at this time. The one thing that is certain is that MRGO was and is a monstrous environmental and economic failure. It would make good sense to avoid such expensive recklessness in the future—but that brings up another topic.

Chapter 9

The Axe in the Attic

*A*FTER A NUMBER of New Orleanians died from Hurricane Betsy, having fled to their attics only to find themselves trapped there, many families learned the wisdom of keeping an axe in the attic. One story about such an axe involves a family that was deciding whether or not to evacuate in the face of an advancing hurricane. After the man of the household had decided the family would stay put, his mother-in-law, the matriarch of the clan, ask whether he had an axe in the attic. When he answered yes, she responded, "Good. After you use it to chop us out, I'm going to want you to give it to me, *so I can kill you with it.*" The family decided to evacuate after all.

One of the reasons why such stories are so common is that there are so many cases where the endings have not been happy ones. The title for the collection of post-Katrina stories by one of the best-loved columnists of the *New Orleans Times-Picayune*, Chris Rose, was *1 Dead in Attic*—a tribute to Thomas Coleman, a retired longshoreman who did in fact die in his attic. As was the case for so many other victims, his body was eventually found by recovery workers, who recorded what they found, in spray paint, on the outside of his house. By contrast, a few miles to the southeast of New Orleans, the nephew of the official from Plaquemines Parish who was mentioned in Chapter 1—a man who had no such axe in his attic, but who some-

Escape route from rapidly flooding attic, as cut by butcher knife while storm waters continued to rise (see left side of roof, near the top). Photograph by Robert Gramling.

how had the presence of mind to grab a butcher knife on his way up the stairs, when the rapidly rising flood waters chased him off the tops of the kitchen cabinets—managed to chop his way to freedom through a hole in the roof.[1]

Those of us who live in other states may be tempted to take comfort from the view that the drowning of New Orleans might be just as "unique" to Louisiana as Mardi Gras parades, Creole cuisine, or the origins of jazz. Assumptions can be comforting, however, without being accurate. Another possibility is that, in part through their experiences, the people of the New Orleans region may have learned a thing or two, and that the rest of us might benefit by learning from them in turn.

In a broader sense, after all, Katrina was not "the big one." It was an early if deadly warning for the rest of us. Like the proverbial canary in the coal mine—useful for warnings in part precisely because of its pronounced vulnerabilities—New Orleans has provided an experience that we can interpret as isolated, or one that we can understand as being informative. In this chapter, we consider a pair of examples from different parts of the country, both of which suggest that seeing the un-natural disaster in New Orleans as an isolated exception would not be the wisest course of action.

California's Delta Blues

We turn first to America's second-largest population living below sea level, and its fastest-growing one. To the surprise of many, it is located more than half a continent to the west of New Orleans, in the California Delta.

Like the delta in Louisiana, this one has been built up over thousands of years, albeit by two main rivers—the Sacramento River, from the north, and the San Joaquin, from the south—along with an assortment of smaller ones. The California Delta is shaped a bit like a triangle that has been squeezed by a vise. Its point aims westward, toward San Francisco Bay, but its eastern edge is more than 30 miles inland from there, stretching more than 60 miles from north to south, roughly from Sacramento to Stockton.

As in the case of the Mississippi River Delta, this is an area of rich soils. As farmers drained those soils in the interest of raising crops, they and their descendants eventually built more than a thousand miles of levees to protect what they called "islands"—a name that soon became more and more ironic. As was the case in New Orleans, once the soils dried out, the land sank. Oxygen got to the rich organic deposits, and microbes went to work, turning the carbon in those deposits into carbon dioxide. The process has been so effective that, today, many of the "islands" are twenty or more feet below sea level.

California gets far less rain than Louisiana, but the rain it does get will often come in the form of major, even world-class storms. It also gets earthquakes. Neither of these facts could be called a closely guarded secret, but neither seems to have received much attention until recently. Unfortunately, when geologists did a simple study that took these two facts into account—using simple calculations, extrapolated from well-established trends—they found roughly a two-thirds probability that major sections of the California Delta will be taken over by Pacific Ocean waters within the next fifty years.[2]

Except for the fact that the terrain of California's Delta region is

California Delta scene, fall, 2007. Note that the "Island" or land area, to the left, is well below the level of the water, on the right. Photograph by William Freudenburg.

just about as flat as that of Louisiana's, it would be hard to imagine an area that could seem less like the wetlands around New Orleans. It is not so hard, however, to ask whether the Katrina experience might also be relevant along the western edge of the continent. In particular, whatever might be the wisdom of allowing residents of New Orleans to return to the homes they have inhabited for decades, the California Delta would not seem to be the kind of place where it would make a good deal of sense to be building thousands of new ones.

Since 1911, the state of California has had a Reclamation Board, which was created to develop flood-control plans. The board has long had regulatory powers, but in this generally rural and agricultural region, it has rarely used them all that vigorously. In recent years, however, real-estate interests announced plans for building well over 100,000 new homes in this second delta region—often below sea level—and the Reclamation Board, having noticed the scientific findings about the potential for flooding, started turning down the development proposals. On September 27, 2005—precisely

A sampling of the new, below-sea-level housing developments being built (and advertised) in the California Delta, fall, 2007. Photograph by William Freudenburg.

four weeks after Katrina had so vividly demonstrated the risks of living below sea level—California governor Arnold Schwarzenegger created obvious headline opportunities by "terminating" the entire board, restocking it with new members. His spokespersons later assured the public that the terminations had nothing to do with the fact that over a quarter of the governor's campaign contributions had come from real-estate interests.[3]

In some ways, the recent developments in the California Delta offer on-the-ground illustrations of a phenomenon first pointed out over 65 years ago by one of the best-respected geographers of the twentieth century—the man often seen as the father of hazards research, Gilbert White. As part of his dissertation research, White found that the more the United States spent on "flood protection" projects, such as floodwalls and levees, the *higher* were the subsequent costs of flood damage. Even after adjusting to account for inflation, and even well after White pointed it out, this pattern did not end. Indeed, the costs of Katrina, now generally estimated to be well over

$100 billion, will guarantee that the same pattern will continue at least into the early decades of the twenty-first century.[4]

Some of the reasons initially seemed easy enough to understand, with three in particular being widely noted. First, levees and flood-walls are imperfect. An old joke is that there are only two types of levees—those that *have* failed and those that *will* fail.* A more precise but also more serious estimate, which comes from the National Academy of Sciences/National Research Council, is that levee failures are responsible for roughly one-third of all flood disasters in the United States. Second, people often miss this point, expecting floodwalls to provide adequate protection from flooding.[5]

Third, as noted by the U.S. General Accounting Office, among others, relatively extensive research by now demonstrates that levees actually *increase* flood levels. As already spelled out in this book, levees in low-lying areas, such as the deltas of Louisiana and California, tend to dry out the formerly "high" lands they are designed to "protect," as well as cutting off those lands from future sediment deposits, leaving them likely to settle and sink. In regions that are not so low and flat, meanwhile, building a higher levee to protect one part of the floodplain can mean that floodwaters will need to go someplace else. The net effect is that even strong floodwalls can exacerbate dangers, moving them to other areas, nearby or downstream, where walls are not as strong or as high. Other nations, such as the Netherlands, have

* As helpfully pointed out in a personal communication from Edward Thomas (2009), this joke may have greater relevance in the United States than in a number of other industrialized countries. The official policy guidance in the United States, which comes from the U.S. Water Resources Council, effectively calls for levees to provide protection against the kinds of storms and floods that are expected to occur at least once in the next 100–500 years, depending on locations and circumstances, while countries such as Holland or Germany seek to build levees that will provide protection for as much as 10,000 years. In addition, policy guidance in the United States effectively calls for engineering estimates to have a 50/50 chance of being proved wrong by floods that occur within the period for which they are theoretically designed, rather than seeking the higher levels of confidence, such as 90–95 percent, that are more common in other industrialized nations—as well as in many other areas of safety engineering. Those who appreciate high levels of specificity, and any other readers who are gluttons for punishment, are encouraged to consult U.S. Geological Survey (1981) for further details.

been far more successful in reducing floods by reducing the amount of land "protected" by such levees, and instead moving the levees back to leave more "room for the river."[6]

The St. Louis Blues

The pattern identified by White is sufficiently well known that it has a common name, at least among researchers—the "levee effect." Still, there might be value in questioning the implication that this pattern is truly a "levee" effect. The actual causes, after all, are not the levees themselves, but a set of factors that have more to do with humans and political-economic institutions. To put the matter plainly, the damage appears to be due at least as much to the ways in which our policies are designed as the ways in which our levees are built.

A useful case study for examining this point is provided by another region that looks quite different from New Orleans—the area around St. Louis, well upstream from New Orleans, which was threatened by flooding along the Mississippi River in 2008. The floods that year were serious, but they were not as serious as the ones in 1993. That year, some of the most destructive flooding in the history of the Mississippi river basin brought damage to 50,000 homes, the evacuation of over 70,000 people, the loss of dozens of lives, and more than $15 billion in property losses.[7]

In the immediate aftermath of the 1993 disasters, as often happens, there were extensive calls for reform. The Federal Emergency Management Agency, or FEMA—headed at the time by a man with extensive disaster-management experience, James Lee Witt—took the calls seriously, even responding to the kinds of concerns that would later be offered by distinguished risk analysts such as Lee Clarke and Charles Perrow. The federal government, led by FEMA, significantly reduced the size of the "target"—the people and properties at risk—by buying, razing, and/or moving more than 12,000 homes, at a cost of over $150 million. One summary of the effort concluded, "It may have been the greatest exodus of Americans from floodplain homes and businesses in the nation's history."[8]

Unfortunately, the *overall* pattern was something other than an "exodus." By 2005, an article in *Science* noted that this had instead become an example of taking one step forward, then two steps back. In the St. Louis metro area alone, those same floodplains had by then become the location of some 28,000 *additional* homes—more than twice as many new homes as FEMA had managed to remove from the floodplain of the entire Mississippi River Valley over the previous decade. The new homes were accompanied by strip malls, office complexes, and industrial parks, putting well over $2 billion of new investments—and flood-worsening impervious surfaces—on what had formerly been thousands of acres of flood-absorbing bottomlands, which just happen to have been under 10–15 feet of water in the 1993 floods. The new developments amounted to more building in the floodplain than had occurred in the entire previous history of the state. Only time will tell if the new developments will stay above water the next time the region sees water levels as high or higher than those that were experienced in 1993.[9]

According to some of the economists with whom we have discussed this pattern, what took place in the Mississippi River Valley over that 15-year period was simply the capturing of "rents"—defined by the noted economist David Ricardo, near the start of the nineteenth century, as the economic advantages obtained by putting a site to its "most productive" use, as in the advantages of being able to raise crops on the richest of soils rather than those that are merely average, or as in converting that farmland into the location for a new interstate highway interchange. From such a perspective, levee protection has made these specific locations more valuable, and the developers who put thousands of homes and billions of dollars' worth of investments into the low-lying lands in the St. Louis region were simply being rational investors.[10]

Over time, however, "rents" have taken on a more generic meaning, and economists have come to be more critical of what some of them call "rent-seeking." As the term is used in academic circles today, it can apply to anything from the bribes that are taken by public officials to the profits that are can be made by selling illegal drugs.[11]

In the context being discussed here, the term refers to a different and more specific set of profits—those resulting from government expenditures that make land more valuable to special interests, even if the expenditures create substantial costs for society as a whole.

These rent-seeking activities clearly reflect not "market" forces, but the manipulation of political forces. According to one analysis, for example, "The U.S. government does more to promote floods than any other entity," with at least 40 federal programs and agencies effectively encouraging development on floodplains and wetlands, through everything from highway construction projects to farm export policies. It would also be difficult to conclude that floodplain development is consistent with common economic assumptions about equal access to information, although additional information is helpful for illustrating that point.[12]

The Evil Umpire?

At least in legal theory, floodplain development in the U.S. is controlled by local regulations, which in turn are constrained by state and federal ones. In the presence of economic and political interests, however, the devil is once again to be found in the details. The Corps of Engineers regulates some wetlands under the Clean Water Act, but in cases where local governments may be tempted to approve imprudent Growth Machine proposals for floodplain development, the key constraints are provided by FEMA guidelines, under what is known as the National Flood Insurance Program (NFIP). Notably, however, the FEMA guidelines allow nearly unlimited development, even in floodplains, so long as developed areas are "protected" by levees or raised enough to be higher than the previously calculated levels of 100-year floods. At that point, the designations of those areas as posing "Special Flood Hazards" can disappear from official maps.[13]

Technically, so-called 100-year floods are defined as levels of flooding that, based on statistical extrapolations from previous experience, should have a frequency of occurrence of about 1 percent per year. Unfortunately, for reasons that include weather changes, insufficient sampling, calculation errors, and the initially unanticipated tendency for levees to worsen flooding, as noted above, such floods actually tend to occur far more frequently. In the St. Louis vicinity, for example, there have been approximately seven "100-year" floods in the last 100 years.[14]

Still, it is the "official" rather than the "statistically believable" 100-year floodplain that will determine where development is legally allowed. Once an area has been declared by FEMA to enjoy "100-year" protection, then even if the statistically plausible period of "protection" today is more like 15 years—and likely to shrink further, due to global warming as well as the processes of building levees and covering former floodplains with buildings, parking lots, and other impervious surfaces—real-estate developers may be under no legal obligation to inform the people buying new homes and businesses that they are buying hazards at the same time. Instead, the developers are protected by a politically legitimated process that has the same three key components that were working in the case of MRGO—spreading the costs, concentrating the benefits, and hiding the risks.

The *spreading of costs* is already evident in White's work on "the levee effect." All levels of government, and hence taxpayers, have incurred ever-growing costs for building the very kinds of flood "protection" structures that have repeatedly been shown to *increase* overall flood risks and damage—as well as for building so-called economic development projects that wind up doing just as little to help the overall economy as did MRGO. When disaster strikes, the costs of suffering get spread out as well, affecting not just the environment, but also the unsuspecting flood victims—not to mention the taxpayers, who incur further costs for rescues, cleanup, "recovery," and more. The *concentrating of benefits* is obvious as well, with profits going to the very developers who made money by building in places that were under 10–15 feet of water during the last big flood, or to the very small number of politically connected shippers who actually derived economic benefits from the MRGO subsidy of over $1.5 million per round trip.

The *hiding of risks*, on the other hand, requires further discussion. Both in the case of New Orleans and in the case of new building in flood-prone places—which include but go well beyond the St. Louis metropolitan region and the California Delta—the key to the process is a circular "liability crisis."

This is a different kind of liability crisis than has received attention in the mass media to date. It involves a circular evasion of responsibility: those who have been harmed by the actions of others—by the proponents of MRGO, for example, or by the developers who reaped hefty profits from building on land that is highly susceptible to hazards—have virtually no hope, legally speaking, of obtaining liability settlements from the developers who put the homes in harm's way in the first place. Aside from the fact that developers learned long ago the neat tricks of using corporations to limit liability—with the "Rivershore Development Corporation," for example, going out of business after building one neighborhood, transferring or selling its assets to "the Riverside Neighborhood Corporation," which builds the next neighborhood before similarly shutting its doors—the developers will also be protected from liability by other legal walls that are far closer to being watertight than are the levees.[15]

The details can be complex, but the basic pattern is simple. Under the U.S. legal system, local governments, not developers, are expected to bear the primary responsibility for protecting public welfare. Once local officials approve a development plan, the victims of floods may have virtually no legal recourse against the developers. They will need to sue city hall.

When they visit city hall, unfortunately, they are likely to learn that local officials, in turn, may not offer much help. Officials in local governments, after all, are not supposed to be experts on hydrology; instead, they commonly argue that they should be presumed to have acted responsibly if they relied on FEMA's official "100-year" flood maps. FEMA, in turn, will argue that "everyone knows" its floodplain maps are imperfect, but that the agency does not have the money or other resources to redo the entire nation's flood maps. The agency thus passes the blame to Congress, claiming that Congress has consistently failed to provide enough funding for the job.

It may not be that hard to guess the next step. Congress somehow seems able to come up with funds for new levees, dams, canals, and other "pork barrel" water projects, but not for redoing the flood maps— even though improved maps, coupled with improved enforcement, would save billions of taxpayer dollars in avoided flood damage.

The connection to Growth Machine interests is hard to escape. Despite repeated congressional statements of concern over "high taxes," far more taxpayer spending goes into pork-barrel projects than into improving floodplain management. The pork-barrel proposals that continue to get funding, however, are often highly desired by Growth Machine proponents, while better maps, on the other hand, might complicate the development of hazard-prone floodplains.

Unfortunately, while members of Congress may pay close attention to Growth Machine proponents—and to others who make campaign contributions with thick wads of cash—the key details of legislation seem to reflect less concern about the rights of flood victims than do the politicians' speeches. Instead, as if intent on completing the circular displacement of responsibility and liability, Congress long ago passed an important technicality, buried in the Flood Control Act of 1928, that prevents flood victims from suing the federal government over any shortcomings in so-called flood-protection projects. Rather than showing any inclination to make Growth Machine proponents responsible for flood damage, in fact, the nation's elected representatives have made the purchase of flood insurance the responsibility of the individual homeowners and renters—in the St. Louis region, in the California Delta, along the Gulf coast, and essentially everywhere else.[16]

Rethinking Reforms

If there are few reasons to be impressed by our past successes in preventing such problems, unfortunately there are equally few reasons to be impressed with efforts to date to come up with reforms to the system. Some of the most popular reform proposals of previous decades involved requirements for doing formal benefit-cost assessments, but as noted above, the safeguards provided by such assessments quickly proved to be more apparent than real. There may be equally little reason for enthusiasm toward the most popular proposals of more recent years, which have often been built around the argument that government agencies are inherently inefficient, and thus that it would be wise to seek "private-sector efficiencies" by hiring private contractors, rather than having that work performed by permanent government employees. As a moment's thought will reveal, the companies dredging MRGO are fine examples of just such private-sector firms. So are the contractors that sold $640 toilet seats to the Department of Defense. So are the kinds of companies noted earlier as having taken part in "aftermath looting"—getting contracts to haul away debris and corpses, or to nail temporary blue tarps to New Orleans roofs, for 10–20 times the going rate, profiting from the kinds of cost overruns that would make military contractors proud.

To be fair, some of the private-sector contractors—perhaps including the private companies that have won contracts over the decades for the ongoing dredging of MRGO—may in fact be able to move dirt more efficiently than would agency personnel. Unfortunately, that is not the end of the matter: once they win a contract, such firms have little incentive to ask whether all of that dredging should even be done in the first place, and in practice, they have often put their highest-quality brainpower to work not in cutting costs for taxpayers, but in lobbying for increased federal spending for their companies' work.

All in all, accordingly, it is difficult to avoid the conclusion that the primary form of "private-sector efficiency" being seen in these kinds of funding frenzies is in the sheer speed and thoroughness with which the private-sector firms can suck taxpayers' dollars out of the federal trough. As any number of the residents of New Orleans have noted, often with understandable bitterness, the arrangement may have been handsomely profitable for a codependent set of private-sector contractors, but it is difficult to see what benefits such a system could be said to have delivered to American taxpayers—or for that matter to the local residents who had lost their homes, and who were still waiting for the first few dollars of promised federal help to arrive.

All of the above suggests that the time may have come for a different approach to reform—one that takes more seriously the idea of having the government run "*like* a business," rather than just function *for* businesses. After all, before any responsible business would to be willing to take on the potential for huge future liabilities—by building below sea level in California, for example—ordinary prudence would lead that business to ensure that they first have a reasonable degree of protection from losses, as well as from lawsuits. In the past, politically connected developers have been able to interpret "prudence" as one of the main reasons why governments exist—that is, to bear all the costs of risk, at taxpayer expense, and to pass the profits on to the developers. In the future, a more truly businesslike approach would be to see it as one of the reasons why insurance companies exist—while the role of the government is to assure that the insurance companies and other businesses all fulfill their own responsibilities.

The principle that would line up most solidly with what freshmen are taught in economics 101, after all, would be that *the full costs of a project need to be reflected in the price tag.* The simplest way to do that, at least in principle, would be nearly the opposite of the usual benefit-cost assessments. At least to date, those assessments have simply added up numbers, or made them up, but they have done so with no real requirement that the intended beneficiaries actually pay the potential costs of their actions. A straightforward alternative would be to remove the requirement for formal benefit-cost analyses—even thought that might cost jobs for some of our friends and colleagues— and instead require the beneficiaries to pay the actual rather than the hypothetical costs of the projects they promote.

A number of approaches could accomplish this objective, but the key would be to assure that the beneficiaries' payments would cover actual costs to the environment and to the future owners of homes and businesses in affected regions. Again, this is one of the reasons why insurance companies exist.

If the proponents of some future navigation canal through the Louisiana wetlands, for example, really are that sure that environmental damages can be controlled, and if they are right in their predictions that the new canal will bring economic prosperity both to them and to the region, then they should be willing to "invest" in the project by purchasing long-term security bonds, prepaid insurance policies, or other mechanisms for sharing the real economic risk. Similarly, if real-estate developers in the California Delta or the Mississippi River's floodplains are indeed building safe homes, and the geologists are wrong, then the developers of all those new homes should have little difficulty buying ordinary private-sector insurance that would fully indemnify them against any future costs of "highly unlikely" flooding. Even if—or especially if—the developers needed to pay for the full cost in advance, such a safeguard would simply ensure that the true costs of building in those locations would be accurately reflected in the price tags on the houses. If, on the other hand, the costs of buying such protection from private-sector insurance companies were too high for the developers to be able to sell the houses, that would give us a far more realistic sense of the *true* "demand" for new houses in such high-risk locations—well below sea level, susceptible to flooding, etc.—than would any amount of money spent on lobbying and public relations.

In short, perhaps it is time for a new generation of reforms that embrace "businesslike" policies in a genuine way, and not merely as a set of empty words. It may be time to stop putting so much faith in "reforms" that let speculators have things both ways.

Under the policies that have been put in place to date, houses are still being built below sea level in the California Delta—and in flood-prone portions of the St. Louis metropolitan region, and in hundreds of other such locations, all across America—because the policies of the past have made it cheaper *for the developers* to build in those locations. Such building practices, however, have clearly not been "cheap," economically rational, or good for the broader economy, under any sensible ways of thinking about the matter. The practices, instead, have proved to be costly indeed, both for the overall economy and for taxpayers, who have paid at least twice—once for building levees or canals in locations where they actually make little sense, then again in picking up the costs of rescue and recovery.

Such policies have also been profoundly costly to nature. The damage to nature, in turn, has not been cheap for humans, destroying some of the very ecosystem services that offer the greatest human benefits, such as protecting a city from a hurricane's storm surges, or soaking up the excess water of a giant flood. And past approaches have most certainly not been "cheap" for the victims of an un-natural disaster such as Katrina, some of whom have wound up making their final payments, literally, with their lives.

Chapter 10

The End of an Error?

*A*FTER KATRINA struck, it took weeks for the floodwaters to recede, and far longer for the memories of
human misery to do so—if they ever will. From a distance of several years, however, perhaps it is now possible to assess
Katrina's larger lessons.

To paraphrase an observation about the Santa Barbara oil spill
by the same Professor Harvey Molotch who first coined the term
"Growth Machine," what Hurricane Katrina sent surging through
the levees of Louisiana was more than just contaminated floodwater.
Mixed in with all that water and all that contamination was a bit
of truth—not just about levees, but about power, about the ways in
which unequal power has shaped the world we now inhabit.[1]

This was not the kind of power that can be seen in marching
armies—it was far more subtle, but perhaps for that reason all the
more instructive. In retrospect, the power can be seen most clearly in
the contrast between claims about prosperity, which were accepted
almost without question, versus the warnings about pending danger,
which were rejected or ignored.

Even before construction began on the canal that would do so
much to endanger the city, experts warned that the MRGO project
was ill-advised. Subsequent generations of experts warned that New
Orleans was becoming desperately vulnerable. Predictions of danger
that were chillingly similar to what came to pass with Katrina were

put forth repeatedly—some of them statistical, some of them graphic, some of them, in fact, by one of the authors of this volume. Despite such warnings, however, environmentally damaging projects such as MRGO have continued to be described as necessary "for the good of the economy," while risks of environmental harm have routinely been dismissed as something "not to be feared."[2]

In an earlier time—especially during the nineteenth century, when the promoters were mainly spending their own money—the digging of canals probably *did* contribute to regional prosperity. By the time the later canals were dug, however, their actual economic benefits were minor or even nonexistent, while their capacity to create environmental damage had increased exponentially. They may have been built in the *name* of "economic development," but in fact, they seem to have fit only the definition of economic development once provided by a now-retired colleague, Wilmer MacNair: "A set of policies and practices designed to take money from the bottom 95 percent of the population and redistribute it to the top 5 percent."[3]

Given that the decision makers of New Orleans are by no means the only ones to have made such choices, perhaps the first of the broader lessons to be learned from Katrina is that—unless it has somehow been "economically rational" for American taxpayers to shell out more than one and a half million dollars every time a ship made one round trip on MRGO—it is simply no longer reasonable to accept the old assumptions that environmental damage must somehow be good for the economy. Instead, the time has come to recognize that the old approaches were, in effect, a way for Growth Machine proponents to have things both ways, allowing them to enjoy generous taxpayer subsidies for projects they wanted to see, while not needing to pay their share of the cost when their rosy projections proved to be wrong—even spectacularly wrong.

What has actually happened, consistently—in New Orleans, the California Delta, the St. Louis metropolitan region, and elsewhere—is that political and economic systems have worked for the benefit of the few, transferring costs to the many. In New Orleans, in the year of 2004 alone, the taxpayer subsidy amounted to about $10,000 per mile for any of the ships that actually needed all that dredging—and that was before considering all of the earlier "investments," or for that matter, any of the costs of environmental damage or human suffering. Rather than even approximating genuine "economic development," this was a process in which a powerful few were able to spread the costs, concentrate the benefits, and hide the risks.

A second lesson involves the fact that, even for the few, the benefits proved to be surprisingly modest. In New Orleans, local Growth Machine interests failed to recognize the implications of historical trends toward ever-larger vessels. This simple failure, coupled with the fact that the period of active lobbying for MRGO stretched over four decades, meant that MRGO was nearly obsolete by the time its backers were able to attend the opening ceremonies. In the St. Louis and California Delta regions, similarly, many of the real-estate speculators who expected to profit from so-called flood-control projects instead went bankrupt, even before the new subdivisions were built, when real-estate markets tanked in 2008.

This pattern, too, proves not to have been limited to New Orleans or the other regions considered in this book. Instead, more broadly, MRGO and other environmentally damaging projects have tended in recent years to involve subsidies not for forward-looking or leading-edge investment opportunities, but for some of the very backwaters of the economy. Perhaps economically vital industries have less need to lobby for huge infusions of taxpayer dollars, but the kinds of "water welfare" that have led to so much suffering and destruction have generally proven to be about as helpful for today's economy as offering subsidies to the manufacturers of buggy whips.

The third lesson involves a cruel asymmetry. If the economic gains proved to be modest and fleeting, the environmental harms have come to be increasingly massive—and increasingly difficult to control. In previous centuries, enthusiasm for environmentally damaging projects may have been high, but the magnitude of actual environmental damage was constrained by the limits of existing technologies. Projects such as the Carondelet and New Basin Canals, for example, could be filled in when they were no longer useful. Today, even the Corps of Engineers—despite its usual enthusiasm for major engineering projects—considers the Mississippi River–Gulf Outlet to be essentially impossible to fill in. More broadly, given the remarkable increases that have taken place in technological capacities, ours may be the first generation to have created a world in which the planet itself could be caught up in new dynamics of damage from which we might find it impossible to recover. To be sure, we have developed an increased ability to foresee potential harm and to detect the early warning signals; there is no evidence, unfortunately, that our ability to foresee harm has kept up with our ability to create it. Instead, our technological capacities have now grown to the point that we can do irreversible harm to the people and places we value, affecting our offspring as well as ourselves.

In the opening pages of this book, we mentioned Kai Erikson's observations about a kind of technological Peter Principle. The customary meaning of the phrase is drawn from a book by Laurence J. Peter and Raymond Hull—*The Peter Principle: Why Things Always Go Wrong*. With tongue at least partly in cheek, these authors observed that employees in a large organization tend to be promoted when they do their work well, all the way up to the point where they reach the level at which they are no longer competent. At that point, they no longer get promoted, meaning that, "in a hierarchy, every employee tends to rise to his level of incompetence."[4]

Erikson asked whether the same pattern might hold true for technologies—whether we might have "promoted" the societal significance of our technology, up to and perhaps beyond the point where it can actually do what we expect it to do. In this book, we have noted an additional irony within that problem: our capacity to *do* damage to ourselves and our environment may well have risen faster than our capacity to predict or *undo* the same forms of damage.[5]

The challenge we now face—and the obligation we have to the people of New Orleans—is to do a better job of recognizing and dealing with such problems in the future. We need to learn how to see false signals more clearly, and we need to plan for the future more wisely.

For decades, proponents claimed that MRGO would be amazingly busy, but in reality, its main form of effectiveness proved to be in generating hyperbole, not actual commerce. As should be abundantly clear by now, MRGO was not built because it was "needed" by the economy of the United States, or for that matter, by the economy of

New Orleans. The reason it was built, instead, seems to have involved a different form of at least apparent irreversibility—a set of *political* dynamics that, once in motion, led to the unquestioning support of a so-called development project that, in practice, turned out to be an egregious case of water welfare.

The devastating experience of New Orleans teaches us that, particularly when we are dealing with complex natural-and-social systems that we do not yet fully understand, we need to be quicker to question the conviction that a project will be "economically vital," or that environmental and subsequent human damage are "not to be feared." We need to build our capacity to recognize the potential significance of the harms, as well as the benefits, that we now have the capacity to bring into being—and we need to do a better job of avoiding the kinds of decisions that may prove impossible to undo.

That is true in all realms of life, but it is particularly true in the world of politics. If the drowning of New Orleans is not a sufficiently clear warning to get us to revise our century-old system of winking at the unwise and damaging distribution of political pork, then the question of what kind of "warning" might be sufficient to prompt that reconsideration is little short of terrifying.

Epilogue: Looking Toward Tomorrow?

Under the circumstances, perhaps it is also time to reconsider our use of the word "disaster." It comes from *dis* + *astro*, or "bad star"—origins that come from astrology, rather than from science, or, for that matter, from any acknowledgment of human responsibility. By contrast, according to Aristotle, a "tragedy" results from a mistake, or more specifically the hubris, of a great or powerful person. In ancient Greece, *hubris* referred to needlessly causing shame or humiliation—originally, through acts such as mutilating the corpse of a vanquished opponent, or pridefully challenging the gods and the natural order of things. Ultimately, the word has come to include any outrageous act or exhibition of arrogance. Still, even though the kind of damage that MRGO did to the wetlands to the southeast of New Orleans is easy to compare to mutilation—and any number of critics have charged the Corps of Engineers with attempting to "play

God"—the metaphor is imperfect. In Aristotle's "tragic" pattern, the hubris of the great person led ultimately to that person's *own* tragic downfall, although such an outcome could also lead to the suffering of others.

By contrast, in post-Katrina New Orleans and many other communities, what appears to be emerging is a modern variation on Aristotle's vision, or a triple tragedy. First, the hubris of a small number of "great" or at least politically powerful people unleashes serious environmental harm. Second, that environmental harm worsens "natural" hazards, creating damage not just to nature, but also to other humans and to the economy. Third, in what may be the core of this modern pattern of "tragedy," the consequences will usually be the most severe not for those who have started the cycles of suffering, but for others.

In the end, what has a habit of playing cruel jokes on the poor may not be the pattern that we have come to call "natural" disasters, but the political system that helps to create such disasters in the first place. The outcomes are particularly cruel for those who are least able to protect themselves. Unfortunately, if the ancient Greeks believed that the gods would send punishment to those who most richly deserved it, providing a form of justice, the modern and essentially godless variant is very nearly the opposite of justice. The "punishment" for the hubris of the politically connected few is meted out to the many who are little more than innocent bystanders.

New Orleans proved to be the first major U.S. city during the twenty-first century to experience a truly disastrous hurricane, or for that matter the damage wrought by ill-conceived "economic development" projects, but it will not be the last. Other coastal cities, from Houston to New York, and beyond, could well have later reservations on the hurricane list, and earthquakes or even simple rainstorms could bring a comparable fate to the St. Louis region or the California Delta. The same point applies to the threats that other cities may well soon face from wildfires and rising ocean waters, driven by global climate disruption—or for that matter, to the threats that all of us may increasingly face in a world that we may now be able to *im*pair far beyond our capacity to *re*pair.

In some senses, this lesson was already clear to our grandparents, long ago. They may or may not have had advanced academic degrees, but they knew that an ounce of prevention was worth a pound of cure, or that a stitch in time could save nine. Today, fortunately, at least some professionals offer comparable wisdom, pointing out that investments in environmental protection and in building practices that adapt well to our surroundings can pay major dividends. The National Institute of Building Sciences, for example, has concluded that for every dollar spent on basic mitigation, society saves an average of four dollars—not quite a ratio of one stitch to nine, but a ratio that should be high enough to get the attention of any policy maker who genuinely does care about the greatest good for the greatest number in the long run.[6]

We need to start making those investments. Many of the people of New Orleans who climbed up to their attics to escape the rising floodwaters—only to die as the floodwaters rose still higher, trapping them in terror—had only a few short moments before they met their fates. The rest of us, by contrast, have the time to make informed choices—but only if we begin now, in the relative calm before whatever event may prove to be the next storm. Politicians, of course, mainly receive pressure from politically active interests for making choices that are not nearly so wise, but that does not need to stop the rest of us from working harder to encourage those politicians to make more sensible decisions—and to do so not just in the wake of disaster, but in advance, before the floodwaters come crashing through our damaged systems of defenses.

Even if there is no guarantee that Katrina will be heard as a ringing wake-up call, after all, there is also no guarantee that it will not. The scientific community is not widely known for active involvement in the political process, but wiser approaches to risk management would make rational sense regardless of political perspectives. More broadly, there is no law of nature that prevents us from using the scientific method to do a better job of understanding just how it is that "remarkable" political decisions have been pulled off so effectively in the past—creating profits for a politically connected few, while creating economic as well as environmental harm for the many. And surely, there is also no law of nature that prevents us from seeking more sensible outcomes in the future.

As an initial step toward a better future, then, perhaps the key requirement is that all of us, scientists and citizens alike, need to be less willing to accept the claim that more sensible policy choices are not "politically feasible." In a political system that can be induced to spend well over a $1.5 million in taxpayer money to simplify one round trip by a single ship, after all, it is clear that the limits of *actual* political feasibility go far beyond what most of us have ever been able to imagine. It may well be, instead, that the greatest limitations of the past have existed not in the world of politics, but in the boundaries we have drawn around our own imaginations.

The key story of Katrina, to underline the point one last time, is not one of nature striking humans. It is the story about humans striking nature—and then enduring the tragic consequences. The experiences of New Orleans present that pattern in a particularly stark form, but comparable patterns have appeared with increasing regularity across the rest of the map. Now, however, we have the opportunity not just to watch but to influence the frequency with which such unwise courses of action will be followed in the future.

Today, we no longer live in the world that existed before Katrina struck. Instead, we live in a world where it is not just an option, but a duty, to bring to light the kinds of evidence that have too long been overlooked, and to challenge mistaken conclusions. We owe it to ourselves and to our children. We owe it to the memory of those who lost their lives to Katrina. Just as surely, we owe it to the honor of those who fought successfully for their survival—and if we learn from their example, for ours, as well.

Endnotes

Prologue

1. The comparison of damage estimates comes from the National Hurricane Center's official compilation of hurricane damage and intensity—see Blake et al. (2007).
2. For basic information on the Saffir-Simpson scale, see the National Hurricane Center website—http://www.nhc.noaa.gov/aboutsshs.shtml (accessed 9 Oct. 2007).
3. See Hewitt (1983).
4. The original discussion of the "technological Peter Principle" was provided by Erikson (1976).
5. See Kelman (2005) and Lewis (2003, 19–20); see also Kolb (2006).

Chapter One

1. The numbers come from Shallat (2000, 122); see also Colten and Welch (2003, 3).
2. For more details, see Davis (1990), as well as Blake et al. (2007).
3. See Freudenburg and Gramling (1994).
4. CBS News (2005); Ripley (2006).
5. The most vivid of the bulletins were issued by Robert Ricks, from the Slidell office of the National Weather Service, on Sunday, August 28. See Schleifstein (2006); for original text, see http://www.srh.noaa.gov/data/warn_archive/LIX/NPW/0828_155101.txt (accessed 19 Oct. 2008).
6. The statement has since been removed from Corps websites, but see for example O'Driscoll et al. (2005).
7. For notable assessments of this point by knowledgeable disaster researchers, see, for example, Clarke (1993) and Tierney (2003).
8. See, for example, Dwyer and Drew (2005).
9. The account was distributed widely available on the internet and is still available in many locations. These quotations are drawn from http://www.emsnetwork.org/cgi?bin/artman/exec/view.cgi?archive=56&num=18427 (accessed 14 Mar. 2007).
10. One of the clearest accounts of the efforts by the Coast Guard is provided by Ripley (2005).
11. For additional discussion, see McQuaid and Schleifstein (2006, 54).
12. Quarantelli's quote is reported in Walker (2005).
13. See, for example, the account by Yen (2005).
14. See, for example, the account by Hedges (2005).

15. These quotations come from the story in the *Washington Post* by Glasser and Grunwald (2005).
16. The quotation is from Glasser and Grunwald (2005).

Chapter Two

1. For further information on the "working coast" of Louisiana, and the statistics in this paragraph, see Gramling and Hagelman (2005), as well as Gramling (1996).
2. For a more extensive description of the process, see, for example, Saucire (1994).
3. The information on silt loads comes from U.S. National Park Service (1997). The nineteenth-century quotation comes from *Planters' Banner*, 1848. For a more extensive discussion, see Gramling and Freudenburg (1996).
4. Kesel (1988) found that there has been a decrease of more than 80 percent in the amount of suspended sediment transported by the lower Mississippi River below Tarbert Landing, Mississippi, from 1851 to 1982. For further information, see U.S. Geological Survey (2007), as well as Keown et al. (1986) and Meade et al. (1990).
5. For more on this period of history in the region, see Tebeau (1971).
6. For further discussion on the original selection of the city's location, and other, potentially competing sites, see especially Campanella (2002).
7. The quotation is from Lewis (2003, 9).
8. For a more extensive discussion of the origins of the Cajuns, see, for example, Kniffen (1968).
9. For further discussion, see, for example, Gramling and Hagelman (2005).
10. See Giraud (1990) for more discussion of the region's rich history of ethnic interchange.
11. For more details, again see Kniffen (1968).
12. One of the best descriptions of the settlements of the Louisiana deltaic plain is provided by Davis (1992).
13. For more on the Cajun spirit, see especially Gramling, Forsyth, and Mooney (1987).

Chapter Three

1. See Spitzer (1985).
2. The quotation is from Stoddard (1974, 163); see also Campanella (2002).
3. The quotation is from Paxton (1822, 37).
4. For an insightful analysis of this pattern, see especially Gilmore (1944).
5. See Stoddard (1974); also Campanella (2002).
6. For more on the construction of the "New Basin Canal," see Campanella (2002).
7. See Dabney (1921); also Jackson (1997).
8. Campanella (2002). His comparisons are presented on page 68.

9. For more on Fulton and his steamboat, see especially Foster (1989).
10. Hunter (1949, 66).
11. The official source of statistics showing this to be the nation's busiest port complex is the U.S. Bureau of Transportation Statistics (2007). See also Schill (1974), Steigman (1971), and Azcona (2006).

Chapter Four

1. For an extensive discussion of Lafitte and his activities, see Ramsay (1996).
2. See especially Molotch (1976); see also Logan and Molotch (1987).
3. For widely accepted academic arguments that treat environmental harm as being necessary for economic expansion, see, for example, Schnaiberg (1980), Catton (1980), and Dunlap (1993); see also O'Connor (1991).
4. For further discussion, see especially Freudenburg (2005, 2006); see also Nowak, Bowen, and Cabot (2006); Freudenburg, Berry, and Howell (2007).
5. The quotation is taken from the online version of the encyclopedia, which also provides a useful summary of the history of canals: http://www. answers.com/main/ntquery?s=Canal&method=2&gwp=13 (accessed 12 Feb. 2007).
6. McQuaid and Schleifstein (2006, 62).
7. Kelman (2003, 148).
8. "NEW LAKE BORGNE CANAL; Will Have Important Bearing on St. Louis and Chicago Lumber Business." *New York Times* (24 Nov. 1900). See http://www.nytimes.com/mem/archive-free/pdf?_r=1&res=9502E2D 7153FE433A25757C2A9679D946197D6CF&oref=slogin (accessed 29 May 2008).
9. For details, see especially Ciccantell and Bunker (2002) and Bunker and Ciccantell (1995); see also Sasaki (1976).

Chapter Five

1. Azcona (2006); the quotation is from page 79.
2. Louisiana General Assembly (1896), as quoted in Kelman (2003, 143). See also Azcona (2006, 79).
3. Azcona (2006).
4. Dabney (1921). The quotation is taken from page 5.
5. Dabney (1921). The quotations are taken from pages 9–10.
6. Bolding (1969); see also Dabney (1921).
7. The map is from U.S. Army Corps of Engineers *Flood Control and Navigation Maps: Mississippi River Below Hannibal, Missouri to the Gulf of Mexico* (1989). Drawing on original records, Bolding (1969) reported that approximately $70 million worth of industries had located along the channel by the mid-1960s.
8. For an excellent analysis of Higgins's efforts, see Youngman (2009). The plant has long since become the location for NASA's Michaud facility.

9. Board of Commissioners for the Port of New Orleans (1921). The quotations are from page 19. We thank Dave Rogers for bringing this pamphlet to our attention.

10. The quotation is from the *Eureka News Bulletin* (1942, 14), as quoted by Youngman (2009). For other detailed analyses of local efforts to develop "seaways" during this era, see also Bolding (1966, 1969).

11. Azcona (2006); the quotations are from page 87. See also Board of Commissioners of the Port of New Orleans (1950) and Juhn (1967).

12. For more-detailed discussions of the early history and significance of national-level funding of water projects, see especially O'Neill (2006); see also Reisner (1993).

13. The classic discussion is by McPhee (1989). See also Gomez (2000).

14. For useful overviews of the history of cost-benefit assessment, see Hammond (1966); also Boardman et al. (2006).

15. The first quotation is from Alperin (1983, 32–34); the emphasis has been added. The declaration from the Chief of Engineers is from the U.S. House of Representatives (1936), as quoted in U.S. House of Representatives (1951, 19).

16. *New Orleans Item*, 27 July 1943, page 21, as quoted in Azcona (2006, 24).

17. Bolding (1969, 53).

18. The quotation comes from U.S. House of Representatives (1951, 7).

19. U.S. House of Representatives (1951, 42).

20. The governor's assessment is quoted in U.S. Army Corps of Engineers (2007a, 3). See also U.S. House of Representatives (1951).

21. The quotations, as well as the calculations, are from U.S. House of Representatives (1951). The key dollar amounts are reported on pages 14–15.

22. Hoos (1979); the quotation is from pages 195–96.

23. U.S. House of Representatives (1951). The discussion of turnaround time and "relief of congestion" is on page 2, the quotation about the "aversion to locks and side channels" is from page 12, and the reference to "dense" fog is on page 30.

24. U.S. House of Representatives (1951); the quotation is from page 3. As we will discuss below, this new lock was never built, although it would continue to be the focus of controversy, up to and past the arrival of Katrina. At that earlier time, however, the proposal to build the new lock was enough for Director Statts.

25. Bolding (1969). The quotation is from page 58.

26. *Times-Picayune* editorial, 10 Dec. 1957.

27. The $580 million estimate includes direct costs of construction, operation, and maintenance of MRGO, as reported in U.S. Army Corps of Engineers (2008)—the Engineering Appendix of the agency's Final MRGO Report to Congress. The 1958 starting date is listed in U.S. Army Corps of Engineers (1965, 527).

28. Louisiana Wildlife and Fisheries Commission (1957). The quotations are all from pages 1–5. The Commission also noted that the proposed project would ruin over 100,000 waterfowl hunts and 1,000,000 fishing trips per year—and perhaps to show that it was opposed merely to the environmentally damaging route that had been selected by the Corps, rather than to the idea of a new navigation channel, the commission even identified a pair of alternative routes that would have been far less destructive to the fish and wildlife resources of southeastern Louisiana.

29. The summary of the letter is provided by Brown (2006b).

30. U.S. Fish and Wildlife Service (1958). The fact that this was an "interim" report may or may not be telling. What is clear is that the cover page bears the additional designation, "PRELIMINARY DRAFT OF PROPOSED REPORT SUBJECT TO REVISION NOT FOR PUBLIC RELEASE." As noted in the text, we have been unable to locate a "final" version of the report. Special thanks are due to Rex Caffey and especially Mark Schexnayder of Louisiana State University for preserving the "draft" document. The quotations on "major ecological change" are drawn from pages 24–25; the more specific figures are reported on pages 6–9.

31. The quotation is from page 1 of the *St. Bernard Voice*, 22 Nov. 1957. The population figures are from the U.S. Census Bureau.

32. *St. Bernard Voice* (13 Dec. 1957).

33. *St. Bernard Voice* (6 Dec. 1957).

34. *St. Bernard Voice* (13 Dec. 1957).

35. Brown (2006a).

Chapter Six

1. The construction included four main stages. The first stage involved enlarging the existing Gulf Intracoastal Waterway (GIWW) between the Paris Road Bridge and the Industrial Canal—the new "Inner Harbor"—by removing approximately 20 million cubic yards of soil. The second stage, involving an additional 27 million cubic yards, dredged an initial access channel between the GIWW and Breton Sound. Using the access channel, the third and fourth stages removed an additional 225 million cubic yards of dredge material to reach the final project dimensions—a channel 36 feet deep with a bottom width of 500 feet. MRGO was officially declared to be finished in January 1968, roughly ten years after construction first began. For more on the history, see Campanella (2002) and Brown (2006a); see also Day (2005).

2. In the case of the 17th Street Canal, for example, the interlocking pilings were driven about 12–14 feet into the ground. The concrete walls were formed around the tops of the pilings, which protruded just another couple of feet above the soil, with the tops of the concrete portions of the walls extending to about 8 feet above the surrounding soil.

3. See Independent Levee Investigation Team (2006b); see also Bea (2006).
4. The first report on the damage to this stretch of the levee system to appear in the mass media was also the first to provide the basic argument from the Corps—see Vartabedian and Pae (2005).
5. For flood depth estimates, see Mashriqui et al. (2006) and U.S. Army Corps of Engineers (2006a). For the first newspaper story reporting the account from the Corps, see Vartabedian and Pae (2005).
6. See the report by MacCash and Byrne (2005).
7. See Jonkman et al. (2009).
8. There are numerous accounts of Hurricane Betsy; for a simple online summary, see http://www.answers.com/main/ntquery?s=hurricane+betsy&m ethod=2&gwp=13 (accessed 12 Sept. 2005).
9. See Knabb et al. (2005).
10. Hurricane Camille has also been the focus of numerous reports, including *Hurricane Camille: Storm of the Century*, as well as NOAA's *Deadliest US Hurricanes*. For a straightforward summary readily available on the Web, see http://www.answers.com/main/ntquery?s=hurricane+camille&metho d=2&gwp=13 (accessed 28 Sept. 2005).

Chapter Seven

1. For the perspective from Corps officials, see especially U.S. Army Corps of Engineers (2006a); see also U.S. Army Corps of Engineers 2007b).
2. Anderson et al. (2007).
3. The editorial was printed in *New Orleans Times-Picayune*, 19 June 2007. See http://www.nola.com/news/t-p/editorials/index.ssf?/base/news-4/ 1182230785208490.xml&coll=1 (accessed 9 Aug. 2007). For a story on the information from Levees.org, see Shaban (2008).
4. Some of the key independent reports, which provide some of the information being summarized here, include work by the National Science Foundation's Independent Levee Investigation Team (2006a and 2006b), Mashriqui et al. (2006), and van Heerden (2006).
5. U.S. Army Corps of Engineers (2007b). The quotation is taken from Appendix D: D-E1-3.
6. U.S. Army Corps of Engineers (2007b), Appendix D. Quotation is from page D-1.
7. The official compilation from the U.S. Geological Service is Barras et al. (2004); specific land loss totals are reported on page 4. The most careful compilation we have found is by Saffer et al. (in press). See also Louisiana Coastal Wetlands Conservation and Restoration Task Force and the Wetlands Conservation and Restoration Authority (1998).
8. The statistics are drawn from the compilation by Barras et al (2004); see also U.S. Geological Survey (2006).
9. For a more detailed discussion, see Gramling (1996).
10. Brown (2006a, A1).

11. Azcona, "Grow They Must" (2006). For a more detailed discussion of the effects of salinity on freshwater wetlands, see Shaffer et al. (in press).

12. For the original report containing Gagliano's findings, see Coastal Environments Inc. (1972); see also U.S. District Court, Eastern District of Louisiana (2008). For Corps findings, see U.S. Army Corps of Engineers (1999), as cited in Caffey and Leblanc (2002) and in Carter and Stern (2006).

13. Kerlin (1979). Caffey and Leblanc (2002).

14. U.S. Army Corps of Engineers (2004a). The quotation is from page MR 4.18.

15. The quotation is from page 2 of Caffey and Leblanc (2002). The official Corps report on "de-authorizing" MRGO (U.S. Army Corps of Engineers, 2007a, 2007b) acknowledges that the effects of MRGO even extend to Lake Pontchartrain, which lies to the north of New Orleans. Prior to construction of the MRGO, typical tidal flow within the Breton Sound area was reduced as it moved across the marshes and wetlands inward toward Lake Borgne (U.S. Army Corps of Engineers, 2004a). The Bayou La Loutre ridge provided a basin boundary that limited the flow of saline water from the Breton Sound area into Lake Borgne (Shaffer et al., in press), but MRGO provided a more direct flow of saltier, stratified water, which sinks to the bottom of Lake Pontchartrain. The salt water now moves with the lake-bottom currents, and it can cover at least one-sixth of the lake's bottom during the spring and summer (Schurtz and St. Pé, 1984; Lake Pontchartrain Basin Foundation, 2005). This heavy, saline water inhibits both mixing and oxygenation, generally leading to hypoxic (low oxygen) or anoxic (no oxygen) conditions near the lake bottom.

16. Azcona (2005).

17. Coastal Environments Inc. (1972).

18. Wold (2005); see also Grunwald (2005).

19. *New Orleans Times-Picayune* (27 Mar. 1991).

20. *New Orleans Times-Picayune* (6 Feb. 1993).

21. The Congressional Research Service numbers are from Carter and Stern (2006), who in turn base their estimates on U.S. Army Corps of Engineers (1999). The higher numbers build on the later report from U.S. Army Corps of Engineers (2004a) and other sources, as compiled for example in the *Comprehensive Habitat Management Plan* from the Lake Pontchartrain Basin Foundation (2005). Perhaps the most careful estimates to date, from Shaffer et al. (in press), estimate that "MRGO directly caused the destruction of over 21,000 ha [hectares] of wetlands," or over 80 square miles, "and led to the indirect death of far more."

22. McQuaid and Schleifstein (2006, 64).

23. Mashriqui et al. (2006).

24. Hassan Mashriqui, personal interview, 17 May 2007, Baton Rouge, LA.

25. Schleifstein (2008).

26. Grunwald (2006); see also Day (2005).

Chapter Eight

1. The reporting was done by Gordon and Varney (2006). The three general contractors enjoying the highest initial payments were the Shaw Group, Simon Roofing, and LJC Construction, which were paid $175, $172, and $149 per "square," respectively.
2. For the original report, see Javers (2005).
3. King (2006). The quotation is from page 1.
4. As noted by Flyvbjerg et al. (2003), the common pattern over recent decades has been for "megaprojects" to cost far more, and deliver far less, than their backers promise.
5. For the "Statement of Concern," see Louisiana Wildlife and Fisheries Commission (1957). For the hearing cited in that statement, see U.S. House of Representatives (1955). For the benefit-cost analysis, see U.S. House of Representatives (1951). See also Brown (2006a).
6. See the report by Brown (2006b).
7. Grunwald (2005). The quotation is from page A1.
8. Perhaps the most influential of the social-science assessments of environment-economy relationships are those that see what Schnaiberg and Gould (1994) have called an "enduring conflict" between economic prosperity and environmental preservation, or what O'Connor (1988 and 1991) called "the second contradiction of capitalism." As was also noted at the outset, however, we believe that it is important to examine the specifics; in other words, it is important, particularly in the case of the most environmentally devastating projects, to treat even widespread expectations or claims about economic benefits as being testable hypotheses.
9. U.S. Army Corps of Engineers (1997) Appendix E, Economic Analysis E-33.
10. To be fair, at least one of the businesses that formerly used MRGO announced in the first few months after Katrina that it planned to relocate from New Orleans to Mobile, due in large part to the uncertain future of the navigation channel (for details, see Keating Magee Momentum Marketing, 2006). Still, the departure of that business—from a stretch of waterfront that, as noted above, has seen a steady exodus of firms over a period of decades—scarcely seems to represent the magnitude of economic impact that the channel's backers long described. As this book was going to press, officials announced plans to move one of the largest remaining businesses along the Industrial Canal—New Orleans Cold Storage, a poultry exporter—to a location on the Mississippi River, next to the French Quarter. The plan faced strong opposition from area residents and depended on a multi-million-dollar request for an appropriation from the state legislature, but it seemed to foretell even worse times ahead for the "Inner Harbor" along the canal. Most other major tenants remaining along the canal—facilities for a container terminal, a shipbuilding yard, and a

ship-breaking operation—were also leaving or considering the possibility. See Winkler-Schmit (2009).

11. Lewis (2003); the quotation is from page 115.

12. See, for example, Conger and Kraul (2007).

13. The Lewis quotation is taken from page 117. The depth limitations are taken from *Lloyd's Register* (2006).

14. The figures come from the official compilation by the U.S. Army Corps of Engineers (2008). According to that document, the stretch of the Mississippi River below New Orleans carried 305.7 millions tons of freight in 2004.

15. The funds initially appropriated for dredging during Fiscal Year 2004 (FY 2004, or the 12 months ending September 30, 2004) were reported in the FY 2005 Appropriations Hearings for the Corps as being $13,004,000, but the amounts initially authorized and/or appropriated can differ noticeably from the amounts actually spent. The best available evidence on actual dredging expenditures during fiscal year 2004, as complied by the Historian of the Mississippi Valley District of the Corps of Engineers—whose assistance we gratefully acknowledge—came to $19,100,571 (Camillo 2008). For traffic estimates, we take note of the fact that the lock between the Mississippi River and the Industrial Canal has a depth of 31.5 feet. Even in light of the fact that pilots like to have 3 feet or so of water under the keels of their vessels, any ship with a draft of less than 28 feet would not have needed to use MRGO to reach the Industrial Canal, but could have gone through the locks instead. In 2004, Corps statistics (U.S. Army Corps of Engineers 2006b) showed a *total* of ten "upbound" and thirteen "downbound" trips on MRGO by vessels with drafts of more than 28 feet.

16. The figures and quotations are from U.S. Army Corps of Engineers (2007a); both conclusions are reported on page 50.

17. U.S. Army Corps of Engineers (2007b); the quotation is from pages 92 and 25, respectively.

18. U.S. Army Corps of Engineers (2007b); the quotation is from page 20. The Louisiana report is Louisiana Department of Natural Resources (2006).

19. Still, it would be unfair to blame the Corps for all of the remaining threats to New Orleans. To take one notable example of their beneficial work, the Corps has constructed storm surge barriers at the formerly open ends of the London Avenue and the 17th Street canals where they connect with Lake Pontchartrain. Unfortunately, for esthetic reasons, the people who live along the lakefront—whose homes did not flood with Katrina—are fighting the proposal from the Corps to place the pumps at the shore of the lake, where they would do the most good in protecting the city.

20. U.S. Army Corps of Engineers (2007b). The mention of the supplemental environmental assessment is on page 15.

21. For an update on the importance of the lock for local shipping, see DeGregorio (2008).

Chapter Nine

1. Rose (2006).
2. See especially Mount and Twiss (2005).
3. For a straightforward account, see, for example, Vogel (2005).
4. For White's work, originally done during World War II, see White (1945). For updates, see White (1986), Schildgen (1999), Pinter (2005), and Gertz (2008). See also Mileti (1999).
5. For the estimate that levees are responsible for a third of U.S. flood disasters, see National Research Council (1982).
6. For the analysis of research findings, see U.S. General Accounting Office (1995); for original work on the "room for the river" concept, see, for example, Silva et al. (2001).
7. For further details, see, for example, Pinter (2005) and Gertz (2008).
8. The quotation is from Gertz (2008). See also Clarke (2007), Perrow (2007), and Freudenburg (1992).
9. See Pinter (2005); see also Gertz (2008).
10. For a more technical discussion, see Freudenburg et al. (2008).
11. For early and influential criticisms of "rent-seeking," see Krueger (1974) and Tullock (1967).
12. The quotation is from Schildgen (1999).
13. We owe another word of thanks to Edward Thomas for correcting the misleading wording that was included in an earlier version of this paragraph. He is blameless for any errors that remain, as we have not allowed him to see the final version.
14. The number is from Gertz (2008).
15. For a legal analysis of overall patterns, see Thomas and Medlock (2008). For an assessment that sees reasons to expect more rational outcomes in the future, see Kusler (2009).
16. For a readable analysis of the legal issues—and the wording of Section 702c of the Flood Control Act of 1928—see, for example, the discussion by O'Donnell (2008). As this book was going to press, residents of New Orleans and St. Bernard Parish were still pursuing legal action against the federal government for damage caused by MRGO; that lawsuit was being allowed to continue because MRGO was always planned and promoted as a navigation project, not a flood-control project.

Chapter Ten

1. Molotch's original comment was made in the context of another un-natural disaster, namely the Santa Barbara oil spill of 1969. See Molotch (1970).
2. For an example of early warnings, see Coastal Environments Inc. (1972). For examples of more recent warnings, see Laska (2004 and 2005). For retrospective accounts of the willingness to embrace economic development hopes while ignoring environmental concerns, see Glasser and Grunwald

(2005), as well as Brown (2006a and 2006b). For evidence that "megaprojects" tend in general to cost far more and deliver much less than initially promised, see, for example, Flyvberg et al. (2003).

3. MacNair (1999).
4. Peter and Hull (1969).
5. Erikson (1976).
6. National Institute of Building Sciences (2005).

References

Alperin, Lynn. 1983. *History of the Gulf Intracoastal Waterway*. National Water-ways Study, U.S. Army Corps of Engineers Water Resources Support Center. Vicksburg, MS: U.S. Army Corps of Engineers.

Anderson, Kristina, et al. 2007. *The New Orleans Hurricane Protection System: What Went Wrong and Why: A Report by the American Society of Civil Engineers Hurricane Katrina External Review Panel.* Reston, VA: American Society of Civil Engineers.

Azcona, Brian L. 2003. *Regulation, Discourse and the Production of Nature.* Unpublished Master's Thesis. New Orleans: University of New Orleans, Department of Sociology

Azcona, Brian L. 2005. "The Port of New Orleans and the Mississippi River Gulf Outlet: An Historical Critique." *St. Bernard Voice* (22 Apr.): 1.1–1.2.

Azcona, Brian L. 2006. "The Razing Tide of the Port of New Orleans: Power, Ideology, Economic Growth and the Destruction of Community." *Social Thought & Research* 27:69–109.

Barras, John A. 2008. "Land Area Changes and Forest Area Changes in the Vicinity of the Mississippi River Gulf Outlet from 1956 to 2006." Submitted on behalf of U.S. government in Robinson v. United States, Civil Action No. 06-2268, Eastern District, LA. (Dec. 22). See http://www.scribd.com/doc/14300081/barras?autodown=pdf (accessed 10 May 2009).

Barras, John A., Shelley Beville, Del Britsch, Stephen Hartley, Suzanne Hawes, James "Jimmy" Johnston, Paul Kemp, Quin Kinler, Antonio Martucci, Jon Porthouse, Denise Reed, Kevin Roy, Sijan Sapkota, and Joseph Suhayda. 2004. *Historical and Projected Coastal Louisiana Land Changes: 1978–2050*: USGS Open File Report 03-334. See http://www.nwrc.usgs.gov/special/NewHistoricalland.pdf (accessed 3 Feb. 2009).

Bea, Robert G. 2006. "Reflections on the Draft Final U.S. Army Corps of Engineers Interagency Performance Evaluation Task Force report titled Performance Evaluation of the New Orleans and Southeast Louisiana Hurricane Protection System." Berkeley, CA: University of California Center for Catastrophic Risk Management.

Blake, Eric S., Edward N. Rappaport, and Christopher W. Landsea. 2007. "The Deadliest, Costliest, and Most Intense United States Tropical Cyclones from 1851 to 2006 (And Other Frequently Requested Hurricane Facts)." (NOAA Technical Memorandum NWS TPC-5, updated 15 Apr. 2007). Miami, FL: National Hurricane Center.

Board of Commissioners of the Port of New Orleans. 1921. *Outline of the Policies of the Board of Commissioners of the Port of New Orleans for the Inner Harbor Navigation Canal.* New Orleans: Board of Commissioners.

——. 1950. *Port of New Orleans Record* (Nov.), as quoted in Azcona (2006).

Boardman, Anthony, David Greenberg, Aidan Vining, and David Weimer. 2006. *Cost-Benefit Analysis: Concepts and Practice.* 3rd ed. New York: Prentice-Hall.

Bolding, Gary A. 1966. *Efforts to Develop New Orleans as a World Trade Center, 1910–1960.* Unpublished Thesis. Baton Rouge, LA: Louisiana State University Department of History.

——. 1969. "The New Orleans Seaway Movement." *Louisiana History* 10:49–60.

Brown, Matthew. 2006a. "Gulf Outlet Unlikely to Close: But Some Plans Seek to Add Storm Gates." *New Orleans Times-Picayune* (24 Apr.):A1.

——. 2006b. "MRGO Goes from Hero to Villain: Some Want Channel to Stay Open, Still." *New Orleans Times-Picayune* (8 Jan.):A1.

Bunker, S., and P. Ciccantell. 1995. "Restructuring Space, Time, and Competitive Advantage in the World-Economy: Japan and Raw Materials Transport after World War II." In D. Smith and J. Borocz (Eds.), *A New World Order? Global Transformations in the Late Twentieth Century* (pp. 109–129). Westport, CT: Greenwood Press.

Caffey, Rex H., and B. Leblanc. 2002. "Closing the Mississippi River Gulf Outlet: Environmental and Economic Considerations." *Interpretive Topic Series on Coastal Wetland Restoration in Louisiana, Coastal Wetland Planning, Protection, and Restoration Act,* National Sea Grant Library No. LSU-G-02-004. See http://www.seagrantfish.lsu.edu/pdfs/close_missriver_outlet.pdf (accessed 7 Mar. 2006).

Camillo, Charles A. 2008. "FW: MRGO data FY 2001-2005 (UNCLASSIFIED)." E-mail message to Wm. Freudenburg in response to inquiries about amounts actually spent on dredging MRGO, as opposed to "authorized" amounts, which were lower. Vicksburg, MS: Office of Historian, U.S. Army Corps of Engineers, Mississippi Valley Division and Mississippi River Commission. 18 Sept.

Campanella, Richard. 2002. *Time and Place in New Orleans: Past Geographies in the Present Day.* Gretna, LA: Pelican Publishing.

Carter, Nicole T., and Charles V. Stern. 2006. "Mississippi River Gulf Outlet (MRGO): Issues for Congress." Washington, D.C.: U.S. Congressional Research Service, Order Code RL33597. http://ncseonline.org/NLE/CRSreports/06Sep/RL33597.pdf (accessed May 3, 2009).

Catton, William R., Jr. 1980. *Overshoot: The Ecological Basis of Revolutionary Change.* University of Illinois Press.

CBS News. 2005. "Mississippi Coast Areas Wiped Out." See http://www.cbsnews.com/stories/2005/09/01/katrina/main810916.shtml (accessed 19 Aug. 2006).

Ciccantell, Paul S., and Stephen G. Bunker. 2002. "International Inequality in the Age of Globalization: Japanese Economic Ascent and the Restructuring of the Capitalist World-Economy." *Journal of World-Systems Research* 8 (1, winter):62–98.

Clarke, Lee. 1993. "The Disqualification Heuristic: When Do Organizations Misperceive Risk?" *Research in Social Problems and Public Policy* 5:289–312).

———. 2007. "Postscript: Considering Katrina." In David L. Brunsma, David Overfelt, and J. Steven Picou (Eds.), *The Sociology of Katrina: Perspectives on a Modern Catastrophe* (pp. 235–41). Lanham, MD: Rowman and Littlefield.

Coastal Environments Inc. 1972. "Environmental Impact Study, Ship Channel Project." Baton Rouge, LA: Coastal Environments Inc. (October).

Colten, Craig E., and John Welch. 2003. *Hurricane Betsy and Its Effects on the Architectural Integrity of the Bywater Neighborhood: Summary.* Baton Rouge, LA: Louisiana Water Resources Research Institute. See http://www.lwrri.lsu.edu/downloads/Colten_LWRRIFY02-03.pdf (accessed 6 July 2006).

Conger, Lucy, and Chris Kraul. 2007. Panama Canal begins historic expansion. *The Los Angeles Times*, September 03, 2007

———. 2007. "Panama begins canal expansion: The $5.25-billion project will allow huge new cargo ships to transit the waterway." *Los Angeles Times* (4 Sept.). See http://articles.latimes.com/2007/sep/04/world/fg-canal4 (accessed 7 Sept. 2007).

Dabney, Thomas Ewing. 1921. *The Industrial Canal and Inner Harbor of New Orleans.* New Orleans, LA: Board of Commissioners of the Port of New Orleans.

Davis, Donald W. 1990. "Living on the Edge: Louisiana's Marsh, Estuary and Barrier Island Population." *Louisiana Geological Survey* 40:147–60.

———. 1992. "A Historical and pictorial review of Louisiana's barrier islands." In S. J. Williams, S. Penland, and A. H. Sallenger (Eds.), *Louisiana barrier island erosion study - Atlas of barrier shoreline changes in Louisiana from 1853 to 1989* (pp. 8–23). Menlo Park, CA: U.S. Geological Survey.

Day, John W. 2005. "Making a Rebuilt New Orleans Sustainable." *Science* 310 (25 Nov.):1276.

DeGregorio, Jen. 2008. "Lock Is Key." *New Orleans Times-Picayune* (21 Sept.). See http://blog.nola.com/tpmoney/2008/09/lock_is_key.html (accessed 23 Sept. 2008).

Dunlap, Riley E. 1993. "From Environmental to Ecological Problems." In Craig Calhoun and George Ritzer (eds.), *Social Problems.* New York: McGraw-Hill.

Dwyer, Jim, and Christopher Drew. 2005. "Fear Exceeded Crime's Reality in New Orleans." *New York Times* (29 Sept.):A1.

Erikson, Kai T. 1976. *Everything in Its Path: The Destruction of Community in the Buffalo Creek Flood.* New York: Simon and Schuster.

Eureka News Bulletin. 1942. "Canal from New Orleans to the Sea." *Eureka News Bulletin, The Official Publication of the Employees of Higgins, Inc.* 1 (4 Apr.):19.

City Archives and Special Collections, Louisiana Division, New Orleans Public Library.

Fisher, Dana R. 2004. *National Governance and the Global Climate Change Regime.* New York: Rowman & Littlefield.

Flyvbjerg, Bent, Nils Bruzelius, and Werner Rothengatter. 2003. *Megaprojects and Risk: An Anatomy of Ambition.* Cambridge: Cambridge University Press.

Foster, Kevin. 1989. Delta Queen *National Historic Landmark Study.* Washington, DC: National Park Service. See http://www.cr.nps.gov/maritime/nhl/delta.htm (accessed 14 Jan. 2007).

Freudenburg, William R. 1986. "The Density of Acquaintanceship: An Overlooked Variable in Community Research?" *American Journal of Sociology* 92 (1, July):27–63.

———. 1992. "Nothing Recedes Like Success? Risk Analysis and the Organizational Amplification of Risks." *Risk: Issues in Health and Safety* 3:1–35.

———. 2005. "Privileged Access, Privileged Accounts: Toward a Socially Structured Theory of Resources and Discourses." *Social Forces* 94 (1):89–114.

———. 2006. "Environmental Degradation, Disproportionality, and the Double Diversion: The Importance of Reaching Out, Reaching Ahead, and Reaching Beyond." *Rural Sociology* 71 (1 March):3–32.

Freudenburg, W. R., Berry, L. and Howell, F. 2007. "Does the Tail Wag the Distribution? Testing Hypotheses of Proportionality and Disproportionality" Paper presented at the annual meeting of the Rural Sociological Society, Marriott Santa Clara, Santa Clara, California.

Freudenburg, William R., and Robert Gramling. 1994. *Oil in Troubled Waters: Perceptions, Politics, and the Battle over Offshore Oil.* Albany, NY: State University of New York (SUNY) Press.

Freudenburg, William R., Robert Gramling, Shirley Laska and Kai Erikson. 2008. "Organizing Hazards, Engineering Disasters? Improving the Recognition of Political-Economic Factors in the Creation of Disasters." *Social Forces* 87 (2 Dec.):1015–38.

Gertz, Emily. 2008. "Tempting Fate: Fifteen Years after the Great Flood of 1993, Floodplain Development Is Booming." *Grist* (19 March). See http://www.grist.org/feature/2008/03/19/gertz/index.html (accessed 3 June 2008).

Gilmore, H. W. 1944. "The Old New Orleans and the New: A Case for Ecology." *American Sociological Review* 4:385–94.

Giraud, M. 1990. *A History of French Louisiana: Volume 1, The Reign of Louis XIV, 1698–1715.* Baton Rouge, LA: Louisiana State University Press.

Glasser, Susan B., and Michael Grunwald. 2005. "The Steady Buildup to a City's Chaos: Confusion Reigned at Every Level of Government." *Washington Post* (11 Sept.):A1.

Gomez, Gay M. 2000. "Perspective, Power and Priorities: New Orleans and the Mississippi River Flood of 1927." In Craig E. Colton (Ed.), *Transforming*

New Orleans and Its Environs: Centuries of Change (pp. 109–120). Pittsburgh: University of Pittsburgh Press.

Gordon, Russell, and James Varney. 2006. "From blue tarps to debris removal, layers of contractors drive up the cost of recovery, critics say: Top-tier contractors say it's the only way to get the work done." *New Orleans Times-Picayune* (29 Dec.):A1.

Gramling, Robert. 1996. *Oil on the Edge: Offshore Development, Conflict, Gridlock.* Albany: NY: State University of New York Press.

Gramling, Robert, and William R. Freudenburg. 2006. "Attitudes Toward Offshore Oil Development: A Summary of Current Evidence." *Ocean and Coastal Management* 49:442–61.

———. 1996. "Crude, Coppertone and the Coast: Developmental Channelization and the Constraint of Alternative Development Opportunities." *Society and Natural Resources* 9:483–506.

Gramling, Robert, Craig Forsyth, and Linda Mooney. 1987. "The Protestant Ethic and the Spirit of Cajunism." *Journal of Ethnic Studies* 15:33–47.

Gramling, Robert, and Ronald Hagelman. 2005. "A Working Coast: People in the Louisiana Wetlands." *Journal of Coastal Research* 44:112–33.

Grunwald, Michael. 2005. "Money Flowed to Questionable Projects: State Leads in Army Corps Spending, but Millions Had Nothing to Do With Floods." *Washington Post* (8 Sept.):A1.

———. 2006. "Canal May Have Worsened City's Flooding: Disputed Project Was a 'Funnel' for Surge, Some Say." *Washington Post,* 14 Sept. 2006, page A21.

Gunn, R. L. 1997. Project Fact Sheet, Mississippi River–Gulf Outlet, Louisiana, US Army Corps of Engineers, New Orleans District. See www.mvn.usace.army.mil/ops/fact_sht/mrgo.htm (accessed Jan. 14, 2007).

Hamond, Richard J. 1966. "Convention and Limitation in Benefit-Cost Analysis." *Natural Resources Journal* 6:195–222.

Hedges, Stephen J. 2005. "Navy ship nearby underused: craft with food, water, doctor, needed orders." *Chicago Tribune* (4 Sept.). See http://www.chicagotribune.com/news/nationworld/chi-0509040369sep04,1,4144825.story (accessed 9 Sept. 2005).

Hewitt, Kenneth. 1983. "The Idea of Calamity in a Technocratic Age." In Kenneth Hewitt (Ed.), *Interpretations of Calamity* (pp. 3–32). Boston: Allen and Unwin.

Hoos, Ida R. 1979. "Societal Aspects of Technology Assessment." *Technological Forecasting and Social Change* 13 (4):191–202.

Hunter, Louis C. 1949. *Steamboats on the Western Rivers: An Economic and Technological History.* Cambridge, MA: Harvard University Press.

Independent Levee Investigation Team. 2006a. *Draft Final Report: New Orleans Systems,* 22 May. Washington, DC: National Science Foundation. See http://www.ce.berkeley.edu/projects/neworleans/draft.htm (accessed 28 May 2006).

———. 2006b. *Investigation of the Performance of the New Orleans Flood Protection Systems in Hurricane Katrina on August 29, 2005: Final Report*, 31 July. Washington, DC: National Science Foundation. See http://www.ce.berkeley.edu/~new_orleans/report/ (accessed 12 Aug. 2006).

Intergovernmental Panel on Climate Change (IPCC). 1995. *IPCC Second Assessment Report-Climate Change.* Geneva: Intergovernmental Panel on Climate Change.

———. 2001. *IPCC Third Assessment Report: Contributions of IPCC Working Groups.* Geneva: Intergovernmental Panel on Climate Change.

Jackson, Joy J. 1997. *New Orleans in the Gilded Age: Politics and Progress, 1880–1896.* Lafayette, LA: University of Southwestern Louisiana, Center for Louisiana Studies.

Javers, Eamon. 2005. "Anatomy of a Katrina Cleanup Contract." *Business Week* (27 Oct). See http://www.businessweek.com/bwdaily/dnflash/oct2005/nf20051027_8761_db038.htm (accessed 7 Jan. 2006).

Jones, K. R., and H. A. Franks. 1993. Cultural resources survey of the Mississippi River–Gulf Outlet dredged material disposal areas, St. Bernard Parish, Louisiana. E. Search (Ed.), prepared for U.S. Army Corps of Engineers, New Orleans District, New Orleans.

Jonkman, Sebastiaan, Bob Maaskant, Ezra Boyd, and Marc Lloyd Levitan. 2009. "Loss of Life Caused by the Flooding of New Orleans after Hurricane Katrina: Analysis of the Relationship between Flood Characteristics and Mortality." *Risk Analysis* 29 (5):676–98.

Juhn, D. S. 1967. *Growth and Changing Composition of International Trade through the Port of New Orleans.* New Orleans, LA: Louisiana State University in New Orleans.

Keating Magee Momentum Marketing. 2006. "International Shipholding to Relocate to Mobile; Closure of MRGO Is Catalyst." New Orleans, LA: Keating Magee Momentum Marketing, News Release, 26 June.

Kelman, Ari. 2003. *A River and Its City: The Nature of Landscape in New Orleans.* Berkeley: University of California Press.

———. 2005. "City of Nature: New Orleans' Blessing; New Orleans' Curse." *Slate* (31 Aug.). See http://www.slate.com/id/2125346/ (accessed 4 Sept. 2005).

Keown, M. P., E. A. Dardeau Jr., and E. M. Causey. 1986. "Historic trends in the sediment flow regime of the Mississippi River." *Water Resources Research* 22:1555–64.

Kerlin, C. W. 1979. "Summary technical report on MRGO impacts." Letter to Jack A. Stephens, Directory Secretary, St. Bernard Planning Commission, from C. Kerlin, U.S. Fish and Wildlife Service, Department of the Interior, 31 May 1979.

Kesel, R. H. 1988. "The Decline in Suspended Load of the Lower Mississippi River and Its Influence on Adjacent Wetlands." *Environmental Geology and Water Sciences* 11:271–81.

King, Rita J. 2006. *Big, Easy Money: Disaster Profiteering on the American Gulf Coast.* Oakland, CA: CorpWatch. See http://www.corpwatch.org/down loads/Katrina_report.pdf (accessed 27 Aug. 2006).

Knabb, Richard D., Jamie R. Rhome, and Daniel P. Brown. 2005. "Tropical Cyclone Report: Hurricane Katrina: 23–30 August 2005." National Hurricane Center (20 December). See http://www.nhc.noaa.gov/pdf/TCR AL122005_Katrina.pdf.

Kniffen, Fred. 1968. *Louisiana: Its Land and People.* Baton Rouge, LA: Louisiana State University Press.

Kolb, Carolyn. 2006. "Crescent City, Post-Apocalypse." *Technology and Culture* 47 (1, Jan.) 108–111.

Kusler, Jon A. 2009. "A Comparative Look at Public Liability for Flood Hazard Mitigation." Prepared for the Association of State Floodplain Managers Foundation. See http://www.floods.org/PDF/Mitigation/ASFPM_Com parative_look_at_pub_liability_for_flood_haz_mitigation_09.pdf (accessed 30 Mar. 2009).

Lake Pontchartrain Basin Foundation. 2005. *Comprehensive Habitat Management Plan for the Lake Pontchartrain Basin.* Metairie, LA: Lake Pontchartrain Basin Foundation. See http://www.saveourlake.org/pdfs/JL/CHMP/CHMP%2011-18-05%20web%20release.pdf (accessed 4 May 2009).

Larson, Larry, and Doug Plasencia. 2001. "No Adverse Impact: New Direction in Floodplain Management Policy." *Natural Hazards Review* 2:167–81. See http://scitation.aip.org/getpdf/servlet/GetPDFServlet?filetype=pdf&id=NHREFO000002000004000167000001&idtype=cvips&prog=normal (accessed 5 May 2009).

Laska, Shirley. 2004. "What If Hurricane Ivan Had Not Missed New Orleans?" *Natural Hazards Observer* 29 (2):5–6.

———. 2005. "New Orleans, Hurricanes and Climate Change: A Question of Resiliency." American Meteorological Society Environmental Science Seminar Series. Dirksen Senate Office Building, Washington, DC, 20 June. See http://www.ametsoc.org/atmospolicy/ESSSarchivehurricanes.html#62005 (accessed 28 Aug. 2007).

Lewis, Peirce F. 2003. *New Orleans: The Making of an Urban Landscape.* Santa Fe, NM: Center for American Places.

Logan, John R., and Harvey L. Molotch. 1987. *Urban Fortunes: The Political Economy of Place.* Berkeley, CA: University of California Press.

Louisiana Coastal Wetlands Conservation and Restoration Task Force and the Wetlands Conservation and Restoration Authority. 1998. *Coast 2050: Toward a Sustainable Coastal Louisiana.* Baton Rouge, LA: Louisiana Department of Natural Resources. See http://www.lacoast.gov/programs/2050/Main-Report/report1.pdf (accessed 26 May 2008).

Louisiana Department of Natural Resources. 2006. *The Direct Impacts of the MRGO on Hurricane Storm Surge.* Baton Rouge, LA: Louisiana Department of Natural Resources.

Louisiana State University Hurricane Center. 2005. Hurricane Katrina Advisory No. 22. See http://hurricane.lsu.edu/floodprediction/katrina22/ (accessed 18 May 2006).

Louisiana Wildlife and Fisheries Commission. 1957. "Statement of Louisiana Wildlife and Fisheries Commission Relative to the New Orleans to the Gulf Tidewater Channel." 29 May. Baton Rouge, LA: Louisiana Wildlife and Fisheries Commission.

MacCash, Doug, and James O'Byrne. 2005. "Catastrophic Storm Surge Swamps 9th Ward, St. Bernard: Lakeview Levee Breach Threatens to Inundate City." *New Orleans Times-Picayune* (30 Aug.). See http://www.nola.com/hurricane/t-p/katrina.ssf?/hurricane/katrina/stories/083005catastrophic.html (accessed 9 May 2006).

MacNair, Wilmer. 1999. Personal communication.

McQuaid, John, and Mark Schleifstein. 2006. *Path of Destruction: The Devastation of New Orleans and the Coming Age of Superstorms.* New York: Little, Brown.

McPhee, John. 1989. *The Control of Nature.* New York: Farrar, Straus & Giroux.

Mashriqui, Hassan S., G. Paul Kemp, Ivor van Heerden, Brian D. Ropers-Huilman, Emily Hyfield, Young Yang, Kate Streva, and Ahmet Binselam. 2006. "Experimental Storm Surge Simulations for Hurricane Katrina." In Y. Xu and V. Singh (Eds.), *Coastal Environment and Water Quality* (pp. 481–90). Highlands Ranch, CO: Water Resources Publications.

Meade, R. H., T. R. Yuzyk, and T. J. Day. 1990. "Movement and Storage of Sediment in Rivers of the United States and Canada." In M. Wolman and H. Riggs (Eds.), *Surface Water Hydrology* (pp. 255–80). Boulder, CO: Geological Society of America.

Mileti, Dennis S. 1999. *Disasters by Design: A Reassessment of Natural Hazards in the United States.* Washington, DC: Joseph Henry Press.

Molotch, Harvey. 1970. "Oil in Santa Barbara and Power in America." *Sociological Inquiry* 40 (Winter):131–44.

———. 1976. "The City as a Growth Machine: Toward a Political Economy of Place." *American Journal of Sociology* 82:309–32.

Mount, Jeffrey, and Robert Twiss. 2005. "Subsidence, Sea Level Rise, and Seismicity in the Sacramento-San Joaquin Delta." *San Francisco Estuary and Watershed Science* 3 (Mar.), Article 5. See http://repositories.cdlib.org/jmie/sfews/vol3/iss1/art5 (accessed 26 Jan. 2006).

MRGOmustGO.org. 2009. "Frequently Asked Questions about MRGO." See http://mrgomustgo.org/history/frequently-asked-questions-about-mrgo.html (accessed 2 Feb. 2009).

National Institute of Building Sciences. 2005. *Natural Hazard Mitigation Saves: An Independent Study to Assess the Future Savings from Mitigation Activities.* Washington, DC: National Institute of Building Sciences.

National Research Council, Committee on a Levee Policy for the National

Flood Insurance Program. 1982. *Levee Policy for the National Flood Insurance Program.* Washington, DC: National Academy Press.

New Orleans Item 27 July 1943, p. 21, as quoted in Azcona (2006, 24).

New York Times. 1900. "NEW LAKE BORGNE CANAL: Will Have Important Bearing on St. Louis and Chicago Lumber Business." *New York Times* (24 Nov.). See http://www.nytimes.com/mem/archive-free/pdf?_r=1&res=9502E2D7153FE433A25757C2A9679D946197D6CF&oref=slogin (accessed 29 May 2008).

Nowak, Peter, Sarah Bowen, and Perry Cabot. 2006. "Disproportionality as a Framework for Linking Social and Biophysical Systems." *Society and Natural Resources* 19 (2, Feb.): 153–73.

O'Connor, James R. 1988. "Capitalism, Nature, Socialism: A Theoretical Introduction." Capitalism, Nature, Socialism 1(1):11-38.

———. 1991. "On the Two Contradictions of Capitalism." *Capitalism, Nature, Socialism* 2(3):107-09.

O'Donnell, Pierce. 2008. "Beware Section 702c: The Obscure Clause Protects the Government from Suits by Flood Victims." *Los Angeles Times* (25 June):A15.

O'Driscoll, Patrick, Steve Wieberg, Peter Eisler, and Rick Hampson. 2005. "Nation: Inside City, the Deluge Came after the Storm." *USA Today* (5 Sept.). See http://www.usatoday.com/news/nation/2005-09-05-neworleans-holdouts_x.htm (accessed 7 Jan. 2009).

O'Neill, Karen M. 2006. *Rivers by Design: State Power and the Origins of U.S. Flood Control.* Durham, NC: Duke University Press.

Paxton, John Adems. 1822–23. *The New Orleans Directory and Register.* New Orleans: Benjamin Levy.

Perrow, Charles. 2007. *The Next Catastrophe: Reducing Our Vulnerabilities to Natural, Industrial, and Terrorist Disasters.* Princeton, NJ: Princeton University Press.

Peter, Laurence J. and Raymond Hull. 1969. *The Peter Principle.* New York: William Morrow.

Pinter, Nicholas. 2005. "One Step Forward, Two Steps Back on U.S. Floodplains." *Science* 308 (5719, 8 April):207–8.

Planters' Banner. 1848. "A Pleasure Trip to Last Island." Franklin, LA (June 1848).

Ramsay, Jack C. 1996. *Jean Laffite, Prince of Pirates.* Austin: Eakin Press.

Reisner, Marc. 1993. *Cadillac Desert: The American West and Its Disappearing Water* (revised and updated ed.). New York: Penguin.

Ripley, Amanda. 2005. "How the Coast Guard Gets It Right: Where Did Those Orange Helicopters Come from, Anyway? The Story of the Little Agency That Could." *Time* (25 Oct.). See http://www.time.com/time/magazine/article/0,9171,1122007-1,00.html (accessed 6 Nov. 2005).

———. 2006. "Floods, Tornadoes, Hurricanes, Wildfires, Earthquakes . . . Why We Don't Prepare." *Time* (20 Aug.):54–58.

Robinson, Edward, and Jay Newton-Small. 2006. "Louisiana Residents Blame Deaths on Canal They Sought to Close." Bloomberg.com. See http://www. stormsurge.lsu.edu/paperarticles/Bloomberg_Nov01.pdf (accessed 5 May 2006).

Rose, Chris. 2006. *One Dead in Attic: After Katrina*. New York: Simon & Schuster

Sasaki, H. 1976. *The Shipping Industry in Japan*. London: International Institute for Labour Studies.

Saucire, Roger T. 1994. Geomorphology and Quaternary Geologic History of the Lower Mississippi Valley. U.S. Army Engineer Waterways Experiment Station: Vicksburg

Schildgen, Bob. 1999. "Unnatural Disasters: We can't stop rivers from flooding. But we can stop making the floods worse." *Sierra* (May/June).

Schill D.F. 1974. *The Board of Commissioners of the Port of New Orleans: A Recruitment and Administrative Analysis with Three Case Studies of Board Decision-Making*. New Orleans, LA: Unpublished Ph.D. Dissertation, University of New Orleans. Louisiana Collection.

Schleifstein, Mark. 2006. "Katrina Forecasters Are Lauded: Sharp, Powerful Warnings Cited." *New Orleans Times-Picayune* (4 July). See http://www.nola.com/news/t-p/metro/index.ssf?/base/news-15/1151993177728170.xml&coll=1 (accessed 21 June 2007).

———. 2008. "Plans to block surge in eastern N.O., St. Bernard OK'd." *New Orleans Times-Picayune* (5 June).

Schnaiberg, Allan. 1980. *The Environment: From Surplus to Scarcity*. Oxford University Press.

Schnaiberg, Allan, and Kenneth A. Gould. 1994. *Environment and Society: The Enduring Conflict*. St. Martin's.

Schurtz, M. H., and K. St. Pé. 1984. Report on the Interim Findings of the Environmental Conditions in Lake Pontchartrain. Baton Rouge, LA: Louisiana Department of Environmental, Quality—Water Pollution Control Division.

Shaban, Bigad. 2008. "Levees.org founder accuses Corps of spinning blame." WWLTV.com (27 Mar.). See http://www.wwltv.com/topstories/stories/wwl032608bhlevees.300274a.html (accessed 3 May 2008).

Shaffer, Gary P., John W. Day Jr., Sarah Mack, G. Paul Kemp, Ivor van Heerden, Michael A. Poirrier, Karen A. Westphal, Duncan FitzGerald, Andrew Milanes, Chad A Morris, Robert Bea, and P. Shea Penland. In Press. "The MRGO Navigation Project: A Massive Human-Induced Environmental, Economic, and Storm Disaster." *Journal of Coastal Research* Special Issue 54 (2009, in press).

Shallat, Todd. 2000. "In the Wake of Hurricane Betsy." In Craig E. Colton (Ed.), *Transforming New Orleans and Its Environs* (pp. 121–140). Pittsburgh: University of Pittsburgh Press.

Shipley, Sara. 2003. "A Flood of Development: Missouri Lacks Rules on Flood Plain Growth." *Saint Louis Post-Dispatch* (27 July):A12.

Silva, W., F. Klijn, and J. Dijkman. 2001. *Room for the Rhine Branches in the Netherlands*. Lelystad, Netherlands: Rijksinstituut voor Integraal Zoetwaterbeheer en Afvalwaterbehandeling.

Spitzer, N. R. 1985. "South Louisiana: Unity and Diversity in a Folk Region." In *Louisiana Folklife: A Guide to the State*. Baton Rouge, LA: Moran Colorgraphic, Inc.

Steigman, E. S. 1971. *A Thumbnail Sketch of the Port of New Orleans and the Board of Commissioners for the Port of New Orleans*. New Orleans, LA.

Stoddard, Major Amos, 1812. *Sketches, Historical and Descriptive, of Louisiana* (reprint ed., 1974). Baton Rouge, LA: Claitor's.

Swyngedouw, Erik. 2004. *Social Power and the Urbanization of Water: Flows of Power*. New York: Oxford University Press.

Tebeau, Charlton W. 1971. *A History of Florida*. Coral Gables, FL: University of Miami Press.

Templet, P. H., and K. J. Meyer-Arendt. 1988. "Louisiana Wetland Loss: A Regional Water Management Approach to the Problem." *Environment Management* 12:181–92.

Thomas, Edward A., and Sam Riley Medlock. 2008. "Mitigating Misery: Land Use and Protection of Property Rights before the Next Big Flood." *Vermont Journal of Environmental Law* 9 (2, Winter):155–88.

Tierney, Kathleen. 2003. "Disaster Beliefs and Institutional Interests: Recycling Disaster Myths in the Aftermath of 9/11." In Lee Clarke (Ed.), *Terrorism and Disaster: New Threats, New Ideas* (pp. 33–51). New York: Elsevier.

Trenberth, Kevin E., and Dennis J. Shea. 2006. "Atlantic Hurricanes and Natural Variability in 2005." *Geophysical Research Letters* 33, L12704, doi:10.1029/2006GL026894.

Tullock, Gordon. 1967. 'The Welfare Costs of Tariffs, Monopolies and Theft.' *Western Economic Journal*, 5, pp. 224-232.

U.S. Army Corps of Engineers. 1965. *Annual Report of the Chief of Engineers: U.S. Army Civil Works Activities 1965*. Washington, DC: U.S. Government Printing Office.

———. 1997. *Mississippi River–Gulf Outlet, New Lock and Connecting Channels, Evaluation Report, March 1997*. Washington, DC: U.S. Army Corps of Engineers.

———. 1999. "Habitat Impacts of the Construction of the MRGO." Prepared for the Environmental Subcommittee of the Technical Committee Convened by the U.S. Environmental Protection Agency in Response to St. Bernard Parish Council Resolution 12-98. New Orleans: U.S. Army Corps of Engineers.

———. 2004a. *Louisiana Coastal Area (LCA), Louisiana: Ecosystem Restoration Study. Volume 1: LCA Study - Main Report* (November). New Orleans: U.S.

Army Corps of Engineers. See http://data.lca.gov/Ivan6/main/main_report_all.pdf (accessed 4 May, 2009).

———. 2004b. *Civil Works Budget for the U.S. Army Corps of Engineers FY2005.* Washington, DC: U.S. Army Corps of Engineers.

———. 2006a. *Performance Evaluation of the New Orleans and Southeast Louisiana Hurricane Protection System: Draft Final Report of the Interagency Performance Evaluation Task Force.* Washington, DC: U.S. Army Corps of Engineers.

———. 2006b. *Waterborne Commerce of the United States: Calendar Year 2004: Part 2—Waterways and Harbors Gulf Coast, Mississippi River System and Antilles.* Ft. Belvoir, VA: Institute for Water Resources, U.S. Army Corps of Engineers, IWR-WCUS-04-2. See http://www.iwr.usace.army.mil/ndc/wcsc/pdf/wcusmvgco4.pdf. (accessed 3 May 2009).

———. 2007a. *Mississippi River–Gulf Outlet, Deep-Draft De-Authorization, Interim Report to Congress.* Washington, DC: U.S. Army Corps of Engineers.

———. 2007b. *Integrated Final Report to Congress and Legislative Environmental Impact Statement for the Mississippi River–Gulf Outlet.* Washington, DC: U.S. Army Corps of Engineers.

———. 2008. *Performance Evaluation of the New Orleans and Southeast Louisiana Hurricane Protection System: Final Report of the Interagency Performance Evaluation Task Force.* Washington, DC: U.S. Army Corps of Engineers.

U.S. Bureau of Transportation Statistics. 2007. *National Transportation Statistics.* See http://www.bts.gov/publications/national_transportation_statistics/html/table_01_51.html (accessed 21 Feb. 2008).

U.S. District Court, Eastern District Of Louisiana. 2008. "In Re: Katrina Canal Breaches Civil Action, Consolidated Litigation No. 05-4182 K2: Deposition Of Sherwood M. Gagliano, Ph.D." New Orleans, LA: Law Offices of Lambert and Nelson, A.P.L.C.

U.S. Fish and Wildlife Service. 1958. *An Interim Report on Fish and Wildlife Resources as Related to Mississippi River–Gulf Outlet Project, Louisiana, and an Outline of Proposed Fish and Wildlife Studies.* Vicksburg, MS: Branch of River Basins Office, April. (Cover page also indicates authorship by Bureau of Sport Fisheries and Wildlife, Region 4, Atlanta, GA.)

U.S. General Accounting Office. 1995. "Midwest Flood: Information on the Performance, Effects, and Control of Levees." (GAO/RCED-95-125). Washington, D.C.: U.S. Government Printing Office. See http://www.gao.gov/archive/1995/rc95125.pdf (accessed 3 Mar. 2007).

U.S. Geological Survey. 1981. "Guidelines for Determining Flood Flow Frequency." Technical Memorandum No. 82.04. Revised Bulletin 17B of the Hydrology Committee, U.S. Water Resources Council, 18 Oct. Washington, DC: U.S. Geological Survey, Surface Water Branch. See http://water.usgs.gov/admin/memo/SW/sw82.04.html (accessed 30 Mar. 2009).

———. 2005. *Depicting Coastal Louisiana Land Loss.* Fact Sheet 2005-3101. See http://www.nwrc.usgs.gov/factshts/2005-3101.pdf (accessed May 2, 2009).

——. 2006. *Louisiana Coastal Wetlands: A Resource At Risk.* See http://marine. usgs.gov/fact-sheets/LAwetlands/lawetlands.html (accessed 6 July 2006).

——. 2007. *Status and Trends of the Nation's Biological Resources.* Washington, DC: U.S. Geological Survey. See http://biology.usgs.gov/s+t/SNT/noframe/ ms137.htm (accessed 22 Mar. 2009).

U.S. National Park Service. 1997. "Mississippi National River and Recreational Area: General Information about the Mississippi River." St. Paul, MN: Mississippi National River and Recreational Area. See http://www.nps.gov/ miss/features/factoids/ (accessed 9 July 2006).

U.S. House of Representatives. 1936. *House Document No. 46, 71st Congress.* Washington, DC: U.S. House of Representatives.

——. 1951. *Mississippi River–Gulf Outlet: 82nd Congress, 1st Session, House of Representatives Document No. 245.* Washington, DC: U.S. House of Representatives.

——. 1955. *Mississippi River–Gulf Outlet: Hearings before the United States House Committee on Public Works, 84th Congress, first session, on H.R. 6181 and H.R. 6309* (July 21, 1955). Washington, DC: U.S. House of Representatives.

Unified New Orleans Plan. 2007. See http://www.unifiedneworleansplan.com/ home2/ (accessed 9 Dec. 2008).

van Heerden, Ivor L. L. 2006. "Lessons Learned from Katrina and How We Learned Them." Presentation, annual meeting Southern Sociological Society, New Orleans, March 22–25.

van Heerden, Ivor, and Mike Bryan. 2006. *The Storm: What Went Wrong and Why During Hurricane Katrina.* New York: Penguin.

Vartabedian, Ralph, and Peter Pae. 2005. "A Barrier That Could Have Been: Congress OK'd a Project to Protect New Orleans 40 Years Ago, but an Environmentalist Suit Halted It. Some Say It Could Have Worked." *Los Angeles Times* (9 Sept.):A10.

Vogel, Nancy. 2005. "Schwarzenegger Fires Flood Control Panel." *Los Angeles Times* (25 Sept.):B1, B8.

Walker, Jesse. 2005. "Nightmare in New Orleans: Do Disasters Destroy Social Cooperation?" *Reason Online* (7 Sept). See http://www.reason.com/links/ links090705.shtml (accessed 27 Sept. 2005).

White, Gilbert F. 1945. *Human Adjustment to Floods: A Geographical Approach to the Flood Problem in the United States.* PhD Dissertation (Research Paper No. 29), initially submitted June 1942, Department of Geography, University of Chicago.

——. 1986. "Optimal Flood Damage Management: Retrospect and Prospect." In R. Kates and I. Burton (Eds.), *Geography, Resources and Environment 1: Selected Writings of Gilbert F. White* (pp. 197–218), Chicago: University of Chicago Press.

Winkler-Schmit, David. 2009. "Game of Chicken: A Proposed Cold-storage Facility Adjacent to the French Market Pits the Port of New Orleans Against Worried French Quarter and Marigny Residents." BestOfNewOrleans.com

(6 Apr.). See http://bestofneworleans.com/gyrobase/Content?oid=oid%3 A53481 (accessed 8 May 2009).

Wold, Amy. 2005. "'Deadly funnel' of MRGO aided in parish flooding." *The Baton Rouge Advocate* (9 Oct.). See http://www.stormsurge.lsu.edu/paper-articles/TheAdvocate_oct09.pdf (accessed 3 Feb. 2008).

Yen, Hope. 2005. "Death in Streets Took a Back Seat to Dinner." *Seattle Times* (21 Oct.). See http://seattletimes.nwsource.com/html/nation-world/2002574244_fema21.html (accessed 24 Oct. 2005).

Youngman, Nicole L. 2009. "Before Katrina: New Orleans' Transformation from External to Manufactured Flood Risk." Paper presented to 2009 annual meeting, Southern Sociological Society, New Orleans, 3 April.

Acknowledgments

In the process of working on this book, we received assistance from so many people that it would be impossible to be able to thank them all. Still, a smaller number of them have provided so much assistance that they deserve to be singled out here for special recognition.

We begin with a word of thanks for financial support. Several author meetings and some of the firsthand fieldwork were made possible by support from the American Sociological Association, the MacArthur, Russell Sage, Ford, Rockefeller, and Bill and Melinda Gates Foundations, the Social Science Research Council Task Force on Katrina, and the Dehlsen Professorship of the University of California, Santa Barbara. We gratefully acknowledge all of these sources of support, although we also stress that none of them are responsible for the specific findings and conclusions reported in these pages, which are ours alone.

Several people also provided the kinds of assistance that no amount of money could buy. Although they did so largely because they share our passion for preserving what is irreplaceable and historically valuable, they deserve a more public form of thanks than such persons ordinarily receive. Mark Schexnayder and Rex Caffey deserve special recognition for having recognized the historical value of reports from the Louisiana Department of Wildlife and Fisheries and other agencies, dating back to the 1950s. They saved the reports for the first time by keeping them from being thrown into dumpsters, later saving them from destruction again, this time by floodwaters. Still later, they went well beyond the call of duty again, making copies of those reports available to us during what were highly stressful times for both of them. Also deserving of special recognition for safeguarding the historical record is Dr. J. David Rogers, who has written his own insightful analyses of the development of the New Orleans Flood Protection System, and who also helped us to find copies of some rich historical materials.

As we note in later chapters, there were many heroes in the aftermath of Katrina, but we want to recognize two of them, in particular. Nathan Bassiouni and Gaynel Gassert both played roles of on-the-ground heroism in the immediate aftermath of Katrina, and both of them also continued the tradition of protecting the historical record with the unique photographs they took during the immediate aftermath of the storm, some of which they kindly agreed to share with us for use in this book. The tradition was further advanced through the careful sleuth work of Natalie Hunt and Travis Scott, two students working under the direction of Dr. Herbert Wang, from the University of Wisconsin, who put together the remarkable compilation of historic aerial photographs of a disappearing swath of cypress wetlands, which they call the Bayou Bienvenue triangle, just to the north of the Lower Ninth Ward.

Comparably dogged sleuth work was done by Brian Azcona, a master's degree sociology graduate of the University of New Orleans, and Nicole Youngman, a Ph.D. student at Tulane, both of whom have done archival research of the highest order. Brian Azcona was quick to recognize the importance of learning more about the problems associated with development patterns in New Orleans, in general, and of the Mississippi River–Gulf Outlet, in particular. His pursuit of textual evidence, especially in newspapers, brought to life our descriptions of the early phases of advocacy and opposition to that project, and his passion for the details facilitated the efforts of those of us who followed. Nicole Youngman has continued and extended this tradition, revealing new insights and connections through her own important archival research, identifying important details about, and providing helpful insights into, the history and dynamics of the New Orleans Growth Machine.

Edwin Roy, the long-time editor of the *St. Bernard Voice*, contributed significantly to our research in at least two ways. First, he provided us with access to the unique archives from his own newspaper, and second, by generously making himself available for interviews, he provided us with access to the kinds of insights that could only have been obtained from one person.

This book has also benefited from valuable input provided by several professional colleagues in the U.S. Army Corps of Engineers. Given that many of them expressed a preference not to be noted by name, we will respect their wishes, although we regret the fact that this leaves us unable to offer them the kind of public recognition that we feel they deserve. The book has also derived benefits from a number of noted critics of past Corps decisions; especially notable in this regard are Robert Bea and Hassan Mashriqui, within the technical community, along with award-winning journalists, Mark Schleifstein and John McQuaid. One final expert who deserves a special word of thanks for the assistance he provided is Edward A. Thomas. He patiently provided insights into the arcane world of flood risk regulation that were not just helpful, but also sufficiently clear to be included in a book that we have tried hard to write in English.

In the later stages of the production of this book, many people at Island Press provided important guidance and assistance. Mike Fleming was a careful yet good-natured copyeditor, and Sharis Simonian showed a sure hand in guiding the book through production. Still, the most helpful of all, and probably the most patient of all, was our friend Todd Baldwin, who served as the book's most important editor, as well as being Vice President and Associate Publisher at the press.

Just as we thank those who have helped us in the final stages of preparing this book, an extra word of thanks is also due to the other members of the

Social Science Research Council Task Force on Katrina. Those who did not begin as our friends have clearly become our friends as well as our colleagues today. Collectively as well as individually, they have influenced and helped our work in more ways than we can say—some of them starting to do so as early as September 2005, and all of them continuing to do so over the course of more than three years, as they, and we, have sought to clarify the lessons that need to be learned from the Katrina experience.

Finally, beyond all the people who deserve to be thanked for the important roles they have played in making this book possible, a very different set of people deserve recognition for having inspired the writing of these words in the first place—the resilient people of New Orleans and of the broader region affected by Hurricane Katrina. It is to all of them—the survivors every bit as much as those who lost their lives—that we dedicate this book. Our only hope is that we will have performed our roles in ways that, inspired by their good example, will allow us to join with them in helping to make the suffering from future disasters and tragedies a bit less likely.

Index

*Figures /photos /illustrations are
indicated by an "f" and tables by a "t".*

Acadiana ("Cajun Louisiana"),
    40–44;joie de vivre and, 44;
    See also Cajun(s)
ADvanced CIRCulation
    (ADCIRC) model, 115
African Americans, 43
aftermath looting. *See* looting
Alabama coastline, 70; Mobile Bay,
    17, 70. *See also* Mobile, AL
Alexander, Lester F., 73, 74, 78
Algiers Point, 94f
American Association for the
    Advancement of Science, 127
American Institute of Biological
    Sciences, 127
American Society of Civil Engineers
    (ASCE), 112, 127
Appalachian Mountains, 52
Aristotle, 167
Atchafalaya River, 44
Axe in the Attic, 147, 148, 169
Azcona, Brian, 53, 67, 68, 74, 77, 119,
    123, 198

Bahamonde, Marty, 27
Baldwin, Todd, 198
Bangladesh, 115
barge-mounted dragline, 118
Basin Street, 47
Bassiouni, Nathan, 23, 26, 96, 197
Battle of New Orleans, 56
bayous: rivers v., 33
Bayou Bienvenue triangle, 122-125,
    132, 198

Bayou Dupré, 63
Bayou La Loutre, 122, 142f, 143
Bayou Lafourche, 44
Bayou St. John, 37–39, 45–49, 60
Bayou Teche, 40, 44
Bea, Robert, 198
Benefit-Cost Analysis (BCA), 76,
    79–85. *See also* water welfare
Bienville, Jean-Baptiste Le Moyne
    de, 37
Bill and Melinda Gates Foundation,
    197
Blanco, Kathleen, Governor, 19, 28
Board of Commissioners for the Port
    of New Orleans ("Dock Board"),
    67–76
    Policies for the Inner Harbor
    Navigation Canal, 72–73
Bradshaw, Larry, 22, 23
Brown, Michael, 27, 30
Brucker, Wilbur M., 85
Buras, LA, 5
Bush, George H.W., president 26
Bush, George W., president, 26, 29;
    flight over New Orleans, 30
Bush, Prescott, senator, 26

Caffey, Rex, 86, 120, 121, 184, 197
Cajun(s), 41, 43–44 *See also* Acadiana
Cajun Flotilla, 22, 23f, 25
California Delta, 13, 149-151, 156–165,
    168; below-sea-level housing in,
    150, 151f, 161;
construction in, 150, 151, 153
California gold rush, 74
California Reclamation Board, 150
Campanella, Richard, 37, 47–51, 91

Canal Street, 49
canals, 12, 20, 46, 51, 57–65, 69–74,
    92–98, 115–118, 137–144, 157,
    161–165; construction of, 60-61, 65,
    70, 72, 137; discrepancy in water
    levels of, 96; drainage, 92, 93, 94;
    economic development v., 77,
    164; Federal funding for, 74-75;
    flooding of, 91–92; Katrina v.,
    91–92; national security v., 78–79;
    technologies, 61–62. *See also* spe-
    cific canals
Canary Islands, 40
Caribbean, 43
Carondelet, Francisco Luis Hector,
    Baron de, 45–51, 60–63, 165
Carondelet Canal ("old Basin
    Canal"), 45–51, 63; turning basin,
    47
Chalmette, LA, 56, 127
Chandeleur Islands, 32
Cheniere Caminada, LA, 16
chenieres, 44
Chertoff, Michael, 28
circular liability crisis, 155–157, 160,
    161
Civil War, U.S., 43, 61, 74–75
Clarke, Lee, 21, 153
Clean Water Act, 155
Clemens, Samuel ("Mark Twain"),
    65
Clermont, steamboat, 52
climate change, 117, 119, 156, 168
Clinton administration, 25
coastal wetlands, 34
Coleman, Thomas, 147
Columbus, Christopher, 15, 35–36, 43
Congress. *See* U.S. Congress.
cypress trees, 39, 47, 60, 68, 70, 92,
    116–120, 123–129

Dabney, Thomas, 51, 68-70
dams, Mississippi and Missouri

Rivers, 34, 74, 96, 117, 157; sediment
    delivery v., 34-35, 117
Daniel, David, 112
Davis, Jimmie, Governor, 16, 44, 79,
    83
De Soto, Hernando 36
dead bodies, cost of, 136
deadweight tonnage ("dwt"), 139
DeBouchel, Donald, 127
debris removal, 136
Dehlsen Professorship, University of
    California, Santa Barbara, 199
Del Sud, 91
delivery obsolescence, 63–66, 139–140
deposit, right of, 39
disaster(s), "natural," 3–10, 17–19, 50,
    149, 167–169; word origins, 167. *See*
    also tragedies
disease(s), 36, 50; Yellow fever, 50
disproportionality (between eco-
    nomic and environmental harm),
    58–59, 137–144, 149, 150, 154–161,
    164; concentrating of benefits, 156;
    hiding of risks, 156; reductions
    in economic efficiency, 58–59;
    spreading of costs, 156; subsidies
    and distortions in free-market
    systems 57–58, 155, 164–165
distributaries, 44
draglines, barge-mounted 118
Dock Board. *See* New Orleans Dock
    Board
dredging, 82, 85, 93, 118–121, 138, 141,
    143, 158–164
Duplechin, Cliff, 106, 114

Eastbank Public Library, 130
Ebbert, Terry, 28
"economic development" projects, 12,
    13, 50, 55, 56–59, 126, 138, 156, 164.
    See also disproportionality; "pork
    barrel" projects
Eisenhower, Dwight D., 83

emergency response: of citizens, 21–23; of government, 18, 21–22; of U.S. Coast Guard, 25. *See also* U.S. Federal Emergency Management Agency
Erikson, Kai T., 10, 166
Esplanade Ridge, 37
Eureka News Bulletin, 72–73
evacuation: attic v., 147, 148f, 169; of New Orleans, 19, 24; in water trucks, 25, 26f

Federal Navigation Act of 1936, 76
flatboats, 52
Fleming, Mike, 198
Flood Control Act of 1928, 158
floodplain development, 153, 155
floods. *See* Mississippi River flood(s)
floodwall(s), 94, 151–152; assurances about, 102; failures of, 19–20, 21, 96; overtopping, 17, 96, 98–103; levees v., 95-96. *See also* specific canals
Florida, 4, 5, 16, 35, 40, 70, 104, 105, 107
panhandle, 70, 107
West Florida, 40
Flowers, Walter, 67
Ford Foundation, 197
Freeman, A.B., 74
French and Indian War, 39
French Quarter ("Vieux Carré"), 37, 49, 56, 60, 94, 140
Fulton, Robert, 52
funnel. *See* Mississippi River–Gulf Outlet, funnel

Gagliano, Sherwood, 120, 126, 164
Galveston, TX, 16
Garay, Francisco de, 35
Gassert, Gaynel, 98–99, 197
Gentilly ridge, 37, 93
ghost swamps, 128–130, 131f. *See also*

Louisiana, wetland losses; Mississippi River–Gulf Outlet, damage to wetlands
global warming, global climate disruption. *See* climate change.
Grand Isle, LA, 34
Grand Terre, LA, 55
greater New Orleans bridge, 23
Gretna, LA, 24, 25
Growth Machine, 10, 13, 55, 57, 58, 62, 64, 68, 70, 87, 123, 127, 130, 137, 138, 153, 155-158, 164, 165
Gulf Intracoastal Waterway ("GIWW"), 70–72, 91, 113–116, 122–126, 130–133, 141–144
Gulf of Mexico, 5, 27, 32–37, 52, 55, 62, 63, 70–79, 91, 105, 107, 113, 117, 127, 140

Haiti, 42
Hewitt, Kenneth, 8, 9
Higgins, A.J., 72
Higgins Boats ("Landing Craft, Vehicle, Personnel [LCVP]"), 72
highways, 19, 61
Homeland Security. *See* U.S. Department of Homeland Security
Hoos, Ida, 80
hubris, as factor in tragedies and disasters, 167, 168
Hull, Raymond, 52, 53, 166
Hunt, Natalie, 36, 125, 197
Hunter, Louis C., 52
hurricane(s), 4; alcoholic beverage, 116; barometric pressures of, 107; comparison of different, 104–109, 114; conditions of, 18; eye, 18; in Galveston, 16; mechanics of, 3-5; protection levees, 130–131, 138; "right hook" of, 4, 106f; storm surges of, 4, 16, 17, 96–97, 107, 111–114, 120–121, 131–132; storm tracks of, 106f; strength of, 107;

wetlands as protection from, 112; wind speeds of, 4, 16, 107-108. *See also* specific hurricanes
Hurricane Andrew, 25
Hurricane Betsy, 84, 91, 104, 105, 108, 117, 123, 126, 130, 147
Hurricane Camille, 104-108
Hurricane Center, 5, 20, 97, 107, 115, 130, 132, 134
hurricane highway. *See* Mississippi River–Gulf Outlet, hurricane highway
Hurricane Katrina, 4–6, 11–17, 30–31, 87, 94, 106f, 108, 122, 129, 144, 163; aftermath of, 135, 163; beginnings of, 3-4, 20; canals v., 91–92; Category of, 5; damage created by, 17, 18, 91–92, 102f, 103f, 108, 137; fatalities, 103, 134; flooding, 94f, 96, 100f, 101f, 102f; in Florida, 4-5; property damage, 4; storm surge, 17, 96, 97f, 107, 131; third story of, 9; U.S. Army Corps of Engineers assessment of, 20; U.S. Army Corps of Engineers official report on, 111, 114-115; warnings, 148-149
Hurricane Pam, 20, 28
Hurricane Protection Program, 108
"Hurricane Vulnerability Modeling for Southeast Louisiana," 130

inability to undo damage, 166
Independent Levee Investigation Team, National Science Foundation, 27, 96, 113
Industrial Canal, 12, 46f, 65-78, 83, 88, 91–92, 96–98, 100–103, 113, 114, 123, 124f, 125f, 131–132, 139–144; construction of, 69-70; sizes of ships on, 139-140; flooding and floodwalls, 98–99, 100f, 101f, 114f, 131–132; 143f, 143–144; Inner Harbor, 70; lock, 83, 140, 144

Inner Harbor Navigation Canal (IHNC). *See* Industrial Canal
insurance companies, 160, 161
Iraq, 29
Irish Channel, 50
Irish immigrants, 50
Isleños, 40

Jackson, Andrew, 51, 55–56
jazz, 47, 48, 148
Jean Lafitte National Historical Park and Preserve, 56
Jefferson, Thomas, 39–40
Jefferson Parish, 20, 28, 87, 130

Katrina. *See* Hurricane Katrina
Kelman, Ari, 10, 11, 62, 67
Kentwood Springs, 25
Kenyon International Emergency Services, 136

Lafitte, Jean, 55-59, 137, 138, 141. *See also* Jean Lafitte National Historical Park and Preserve
LaGrange, Gary, 128
Lake Borgne, 62
Lake Borgne Canal ("Violet Canal"), 63, 70, 144
Lake Pontchartrain, 37, 47–49, 62–64, 68, 70–72, 92–98; 142f; connecting Mississippi River with, 62–63; flood protection from, 93–94
Lake Pontchartrain Basin Foundation, 127
Landing Craft, Vehicle, Personnel (LCVP). *See* Higgins Boats
landscape engineering, 11
Larcade, Henry D. Jr., 78
LaSalle, René-Robert de, 36
LCU-1656, landing craft, 27
LeBlanc, B., 120-122
levee(s), 34, 76, 117; failure(s) of, 18, 19-20, 96, 151-152; flood levels v.,

152; floodwalls v., 91–96; hazards created by, 152; hurricane protection, 130-131, 138; "levee effect," 153, 154, 156; natural, 33, 40, 62, 92, 93f, 114f; Netherlands use of, 152; protection provided by, 154; sediment deposits v., 152; settlement and, 92. *See also* Mississippi River–Gulf Outlet; U.S. Army Corps of Engineers

Levees.org, 112, 113

Lewis, Peirce, 10, 11, 40, 140

liability crisis. *See* circular liability crisis

Livingston, Robert, 40

London Avenue Canal, 92–98

looting, 24, 135, 137; aftermath looting, 135–136, 158; by Growth Machine proponents, 70, 137, 158

Louis the Great, 36

Louisiana, 5, 13, 15–21, 28–29, 31–36, 40–45, 105; coastline, 16; culture of, 41-42, 45; deltaic plain, 32; European settlement of, 37, 40–43, 60; geography of, 33-34; history of, 36-37, 40-41; resources of, 42–45; wetland losses, 117–123, 125–130. *See also* ghost swamps; Mississippi River–Gulf Outlet, damage to wetlands; wetlands

Louisiana Act 70, 67

Louisiana Department of Wildlife and Fisheries, 197

Louisiana Ecosystem Restoration Study, 121

Louisiana Purchase, 39, 43, 47–49, 51, 63

Louisiana State University Cartographic Information Center, 125

Louisiana State University Hurricane Center, 115, 132

Louisiana Wildlife and Fisheries Commission, 84-86, 137

Lower Ninth Ward, 86, 98, 100–103, 123, 129, 131, 132, 143

MacArthur Foundation, 197

MacNair, Wilmer, 164

Maestri, Walter, 20 21, 28

marine ways, 69

Mashriqui, Hassan, 98, 113, 115, 130–133

Mayfield, Max, 20

McQuaid, John, 26, 61, 127, 131

Metairie Ridge, 37, 93

Michaud, 72

Liberty Plant, 72

Middlesex Canal, 60

Mississippi coast, 17

Mississippi River, 5, 10, 13, 17, 30–37, 39, 44–53, 60–78, 83–86, 92–94, 107–111, 116, 123, 139–144, 149, 153, 154; basin, 34, 45–51, 60–63, 68, 77, 122, 127, 129, 142, 153, 165; Delta, bird's-foot delta, 12, 32–33, 39; floodplains, 154–156, 158, 160; flooding, 34; floods of 1927, 34, 86; floods of 1993, 153–154; floods of 2008, 154; fluctuations in water levels, 62; history of, 34, 35–37; land-building by, 31–35; natural levees, 33, 36–37, 40, 49, 92–93, 114, 143; resources of, 51; shipping traffic, 140–141; silt and sediment, 12, 32–34, 77, 82, 120, 123, 124, 141; Southwest Pass, 31, 140

Mississippi River–Gulf Outlet (MRGO), 12–13, 66, 73, 77, 81-89, 91, 98, 111-116, 119–145, 156–159, 163–167; authorization, 72, 78, 83, 134, 144; authorization by Congress, 83; Benefit-Cost Analysis of, 76, 79–83, 85, 120–121, 137, 160; construction, 42, 50, 66–70, 89, 91; damage to wetlands, 116–121, 123, 128-130; deauthorization and

"closure," 141–143, 142f, 165-166; environmental concerns, 84–86, 88, 121, 126, 137, 164; funding, 60, 64, 74–78, 83–84, 157–159; "funnel" effect, 97, 113, 115, 122, 130–134, 143; GIWW Reach, 114f, 115, 116, 123, 126, 131, 133, 143; "hurricane highway" effect, 13, 91, 112; hypodermic needle, 113, 143; levee, 97f, 113, 130–131, 133f; lobbying for, 81, 82, 89, 159, 161, 165; maintenance costs of, 82, 141–142; Mississippi River v., 81–82, 139–141; national security arguments, 79; proposals, 72, 81, 83, 127, 150, 155, 158; "Reach 2," 113, 114; salt-water intrusion and salinity, 19, 25, 26, 28, 42, 79, 91, 116, 118–122, 129; security, 160; shipping traffic, 141; effects on shrimp harvests, 85, 121-122St. Bernard Parish and, 86, 87, 158; unrealistic design assumptions, 120, 121. See also ghost swamps; Louisiana, wetland losses; Tidewater Canal; water levels, influence of MRGO; wetlands
Mobile, AL, 47. See also Alabama coastline, Mobile Bay
Molotch, Harvey, 57 64, 163
Monroe, James, 40
MRGO. See Mississippi River–Gulf Outlet

Nagin, Ray, Mayor, 19, 28
Napoléon Bonaparte, 39, 40
National Flood Insurance Program (NFIP), 155
National Guard, 22, 28, 29
National Hurricane Center, 5, 20, 107
National Institute of Building Sciences, 169
National Oceanic and Atmospheric Administration (NOAA), 5, 18, 106, 132; Coastal Services Center, 106
National Science Foundation Independent Levee Investigation Team. See Independent Levee Investigation Team
National Weather Service, 18
Native American(s), 41–43
"natural" disasters. See disasters, "natural." See also tragedies
natural experiment, 104–109
natural levees. See Mississippi River
New Basin Canal, 46f, 49–51, 60, 63–64; death toll from construction, 50; Irish workers, 50
New Deal, 75, 76
New Iberia, 40
New Orleans, 5–31, 37-43, 46–56, 59–69, 72–78, 81–87, 92–98, 103–108, 111–138, 140–150, 153–159, 163–170; Battle of, 56; below-sea-level neighborhoods, 95; "bowl" effect, 93, 94; black morticians, 136; Board of Trade, 67; City Shipbuilding Committee, 68; Convention Center, 22, 29; "Crescent City" nickname, 37; Dock Board, 67–69, 72–77, 82, 84, 140; inland location, protection provided by, 16; Levee Board, 84; maps of, 38f, 46f, 59–60, 71f, 72f, 92f, 93f, 114f; Orleans Navigation Company, 47, 48; Port(s) of, 53, 67, 72–74, 77, 127, 140; Sewerage and Water Board, 68, 92; street directions of, 60; Tidewater Development Association, 73, 74, 78; vulnerability of, 11, 134, 148–149, 163–164
New Orleans, steamboat, 52
New Orleans Canal and Banking Company, 49
New Orleans East, 130

New Orleans Flood Protection
System, 108, 197
New Orleans Item, 77
New Orleans Times-Picayune, 84, 113,
119, 127–128, 135, 138, 147
New York Times, 63
NFIP. *See* National Flood Insurance
Program
NOAA. *See* U.S. National Oceanic
and Atmospheric Administration

obsolete on delivery: See delivery
obsolescence.
oil and gas development, effects on
marshes, 118, 124f
Old Basin Canal, 47, 49
1 Dead in Attic (Rose), 147
100-year floods, 155–157
Operation Blue Roof, 135, 159
Orleans Navigation Company. *See*
New Orleans, Orleans Navigation Company

Panama Canal, 68, 77, 119, 140
Paris Road Bridge, 91, 113, 126
Pat O'Brien's, 116
Paxton, John Adems, 47, 48
*Performance Evaluation of the New
Orleans and Southeast Louisiana
Hurricane Protection System: Draft
Final Report of the Interagency Per-
formance Evaluation Task Force*,
111–112. *See also* U.S. Army Corps
of Engineers
Perrow, Charles, 153
Peter Principle, the, 10, 166
Peter, Laurence J., 166
Pinckney treaty, 39
Pineda, Alonso Álvarez de, 35
piracy, 58
Pitot, James, 47
plants, susceptibility to salt-water
intrusion, 118–121

Plaquemines Parish, 17, 147
policy, environment v., 161, 170
Pontchartrain Expressway, 23
pork barrel projects, 57, 138, 157, 164,
169. *See also* "economic development" projects; disproportionality
power, political, 56–59, 163–166
Progressive Era, 76
property damage, 4

Quarantelli, Enrico, 27

race relations, 21, 42
railroads, 61
Reclamation Board. *See* California
Reclamation Board
reforms, 76, 158–161, 169, 170
rents, rent theory 154
rent-seeking, 154, 155
rescue(s), 18, 22, 23, 25, 29, 161; buses,
22-23
resources. *See* Louisiana, resources
of; Mississippi River, resources of
Ricardo, David, 154
right hook. *See* hurricanes, right
hook of
rivers: bayous v., 33; mechanics of
land-building, 32–33
Rivers and Harbors Act, 76
Rockefeller, John D., 56
Rockefeller Foundation, 197
Rodriguez, Henry "Junior," 128
Rogers, J. David, 72, 197
Rose, Chris, 147
Roy, Edwin, 86–88, 126, 198
Russell Sage Foundation, 197

salt, salt-water intrusion, 116–122
San Francisco earthquake and fire,
8
Sanders, Jared, 61
Sauvé's Crevasse, 93
Schexnayder, Mark, 86, 197

Schleifstein, Mark, 18, 26, 61, 127, 131, 133
Schwarzeneggar, Arnold, 151
scientific method, 104, 169
Scott, Travis, 125, 197
Seaton, Fred, 85
security, national, and canals, 26, 42, 77–79
sediment. *See* Mississippi River, silt and sediment
17th Street Canal, 94–98, 96f, 97f
Seven Years' War, 39
Shell Beach, LA, 88, 120
sheet pilings, steel, 95–98, 99f, 100f
ship sizes, and Industrial Canal, 139–141
shipbuilding, 65–69, 72, 139–140
shrimp. *See* Mississippi River–Gulf Outlet, shrimp harvests
silt. *See* Mississippi River, silt and sediment
Simonian, Sharis, 198
site, geographers' term, 11
situation, geographers' term, 11
slave(s), 42, 43, 46, 49, 50, 55, 57, 58
Slidell, LA, 17
Slonsky, Lorrie Beth, 22–23
social multiplier effects, 75
Social Science Research Council Task Force on Katrina, 197, 199
Southeastern Louisiana University, 127
Southwest Pass. *See* Mississippi River, Southwest Pass
Spain, 35, 40
Spitzer, Nicholas, 45
St. Bernard Parish, 86–89, 98, 119–129, 137, 158; concerns about MRGO, 86–89, 123, 126; oyster and shrimp industry, 88; Parish Council, 126; Parish Police Jury, 88, 89, 119, 127
St. Bernard Sportsmen's League, 127
St. Bernard Voice, 86-88, 183, 196

St. Charles Avenue, 92
St. Lawrence Seaway, 78, 83
St. Louis, 63, 152–158, 161–165
Statts, Elmer, 83, 144
steamboat(s), 52, 53; advantages of paddle wheels, 53; sidewheelers, 53; sternwheelers, 53
steel ships, 65
storm surge. *See* hurricanes, storm surges of
storm tracks, 106f, 107
Storyville, 48
submersible drilling rigs, 118
subsidies. *See* disproportionality, subsidies and distortions in free-market systems
Sunshine Bridge, 25, 26
Superdome, 22, 25, 27-29, 47
supplies, 21, 23, 28, 29, 53, 135, 137
surges, storm. *See* hurricanes, storm surges of
swamps, ghost. *See* ghost swamps

taxpayers taxpayer money, 80–81, 136, 141, 144, 157–160, 164–165, 170
technological Peter Principle, 166
technology, technological change, 60, 64, 165–166; in canals and locks, 61–63; in flood-control pumps 93–94;
Thomas, Edward, 152, 155, 198
Thompson, T.P., 48, 68
Tidewater Canal, 73-74, 77, 87; Federal funding for, 78. *See also* Mississippi River–Gulf Outlet
Tidewater Development Association, 73, 74
tragedies, disasters v. 167–168; *See also* disasters, "natural"
transportation: Mississippi River, 51–53; revolution, 19th century, 61; water, 65, 139
Treaty of Fontainebleau, 39
Treaty of Paris, 39

Treaty of San Ildefonso, 39
Treme, 45, 99
tsunami, 4, 8
Tulane University, 74, 98, 99; Tulane
Board of Trustees, 74; Tulane
Hospital, 98, 99
Twain, Mark. See Clemens, Samuel

U.S. Army Corps of Engineers
(USACE), 20, 70–79, 84, 89,
91, 98, 108, 111–115, 120–122, 129,
132–133, 139, 141–144, 198; assessment of Katrina by, 20; Board of
Engineers, 76, 77; Chief of Engineers, 77–79, 82–83; explanation
of source of flooding, 97f; flood
control responsibilities, 70, 75–76,
151, 158; Hurricane Protection Program, 108; origins, 37, 41, 75, 148,
167. See also levee(s), floodwalls
v.; Performance Evaluation of
the New Orleans and Southeast
Louisiana Hurricane Protection
System
U.S Coast Guard, emergency
response of, 25
U.S. Congress, 40, 48, 76, 79, 83, 84,
141, 157–158
U.S. Department of Homeland
Security, 25–28, 91
U.S. Department of Interior, 127;
official concerns about MRGO,
86, 127
U.S. Federal Emergency Management Agency (FEMA), 20, 25–30,
91, 136, 153–157
U.S. Schooner *Carolina*, 55
U.S. Senate, 78; Commerce Committee, 78

University of New Orleans, 198
University of Wisconsin, 122, 125, 197
uptown, 49
USS *Bataan*, 27

Vaca, Cabeza de, 36
Vanderbilt, Cornelius, 56
Vermilion Bay, 32
Violet, LA 63
Violet Canal. *See* Lake Borgne Canal

Waltrip, Robert, 136
Wang, Herbert, 125, 195
water levels, discrepancies across
canals, 92, 95–98; influence of
MRGO 113–116. *See also* Mississippi River–Gulf Outlet
water welfare, 167. *See also* Benefit-
Cost Analysis
Waveland, MS, 17
welfare, welfare check(s), 80–81,
165–167
wetlands, 31–36, 85, 89, 112, 115–123;
insects, 35; oil exploration and
development, 118; protection from
hurricanes, 13, 116, 129. *See also*
ghost swamps; Louisiana, wetland
losses; Mississippi River–Gulf
Outlet, damage to wetlands
White, Gilbert, 151–155
Witt, James Lee, 153
Wood, A. Baldwin , 92
World War I, 69–70
World War II, 65 71–72, 77–78
worldwatch.org, 106, 114; World
Watch Magazine, 106, 114

Youngman. Nicole, 198

About Island Press

Since 1984, the nonprofit Island Press has been stimulating, shaping, and communicating the ideas that are essential for solving environmental problems worldwide. With more than 800 titles in print and some 40 new releases each year, we are the nation's leading publisher on environmental issues. We identify innovative thinkers and emerging trends in the environmental field. We work with world-renowned experts and authors to develop cross-disciplinary solutions to environmental challenges.

Island Press designs and implements coordinated book publication campaigns in order to communicate our critical messages in print, in person, and online using the latest technologies, programs, and the media. Our goal: to reach targeted audiences—scientists, policymakers, environmental advocates, the media, and concerned citizens—who can and will take action to protect the plants and animals that enrich our world, the ecosystems we need to survive, the water we drink, and the air we breathe.

Island Press gratefully acknowledges the support of its work by the Agua Fund, Inc., Annenberg Foundation, The Christensen Fund, The Nathan Cummings Foundation, The Geraldine R. Dodge Foundation, Doris Duke Charitable Foundation, The Educational Foundation of America, Betsy and Jesse Fink Foundation, The William and Flora Hewlett Foundation, The Kendeda Fund, The Andrew W. Mellon Foundation, The Curtis and Edith Munson Foundation, Oak Foundation, The Overbrook Foundation, the David and Lucile Packard Foundation, The Summit Fund of Washington, Trust for Architectural Easements, Wallace Global Fund, The Winslow Foundation, and other generous donors.

The opinions expressed in this book are those of the author(s) and do not necessarily reflect the views of our donors.